MOMENTS ON MY
JOURNEY

RODNEY PERRY

Moments On My Journey: Rodney Perry

©2019 Rodney Perry

All rights reserved. No part of this book may be reproduced, distributed, or transmitted in any form or by any means, including photocopying, recording, or other electronic or mechanical methods without the prior written permission of the publisher or author. Except in the case of commercial uses permitted by copyright law. For permission request write and/or email to the publisher (Rodney Perry) addressed "Attention Permissions" to the email address below.

Email To:

Madeline@rodneyperry.com

Social Media: @RodneyPerryLive

ISBN-13: 9781093864021

ISBN-10: 1-0938-6402-8

Published in The United States of America

THIS BOOK IS DEDICATED TO

The folks in my life that matter. My wife, Angela Perry who has endured me and my BS for the better part of two decades. To my children, Hope, Devin, Rachelle, Raina, Rihana and Roxy, these people give me the air I need to breathe. To my siblings, each one of you are awesome both individually and collectively.

To my Father's, the men that formed the man I am whether it was from doing what you did or not, your guidance didn't fall on deaf ears. Finally, and most importantly to my Mommy, we grew up together. You are missed, thank you for helping me write this book. Till we meet again. LOVE RP.

NOTE FROM THE AUTHOR
Moments on My Journey

This book is a series of significant moments on my journey. Hopefully, you will learn from my mistakes and my successes. Originally, I was going to title this book 100 Moments on My Journey but as I began to jot down those moments that mattered, I realized that there were much more than 100 to choose from. This book is also a bucket list item that I have wanted to check off for some time now. Hopefully, you will enjoy getting to know me in my own words.

TABLE OF CONTENTS

CHAPTER ONE: Home....13

CHAPTER TWO: Early Years....15

CHAPTER THREE: Formative Years....23

CHAPTER FOUR: Things Change....29

CHAPTER FIVE: Coming of Age....35

CHAPTER SIX: I Am A Man Now 41

CHAPTER SEVEN: The Navy....49

CHAPTER EIGHT: The Bay Area....57

CHAPTER NINE: Crossroads....63

CHAPTER TEN: Leap of Faith.... 69

CHAPTER ELEVEN: Welcome To The Business....79

CHAPTER TWELVE: Domino....87

CHAPTER THIRTEEN: The Mo'Nique Show....95

CHAPTER FOURTEEN: Lessons....105

ABOUT THE AUTHOR: Rodney Perry....115

FORWARD

Written by: Celebrity Comedian Mo'Nique

What can I say about Rodney Perry. First and foremost, I love playing with him. We are just kids with grown up faces. He has been consistently consistent. From the comedy stages where he is the consummate professional, to the Television studio where he was and still is my Right-hand man. Rodney is a complete comedian Father and Friend. I have had a chance to live with him through some of his moments and I'm anxious to learn about the others.

Most people know Rp as a snappy dresser he will put some colors together that on a lesser man would be challenged. I always thought he was just brave, until one day we were preparing for the "Mo'Nique in the Afternoon Radio Show" when Rodney shared with all of us in the studio that he was color blind. It all made sense. Yes, he was still brave be he had no idea his colors were clashing. We all laughed.

The most impressive thing about Rodney Perry is his character. We were doing a show in Chicago, an annual show for me. Rodney said something that managed to offend the entire crowd. He took it in stride and finished the set. The aftermath was even worse people were writing emails. Not sure what he said but they were pissed. As far as I was concerned it was over but Rodney, not to be outdone reached out to the events promoter and volunteered to come back the following year at his own expense. The promoter was impressed and so was I. You cannot teach character and Rodney Perry has it is by the boat loads. I'm sure you all will enjoy taking this Journey with my Friend.

CHAPTER ONE

Home

My mother is Venice Celeste Hunt. My biological father is Leo Jordan. My mother fell in love with my father. He was a grown man. He was married with children. My mother was friends with his eldest stepdaughter. They became romantically involved and I was a result of that relationship. Uh, because of that, my siblings from my father's side and I were never really in touch. That was until recently, after his wife's passing. It was me and my mommy. When I tell the story, I like to stop and acknowledge Benjamin Perry. Benjamin Perry, to me, is probably the most awesome of my Dad's. I say Dad's plural because of course, the DNA that surges through my veins comes from Leo Jordan. My facial appearance, my looks, my demeanor. Benjamin Perry did something that men of any kind often don't do.

Benjamin Perry was in love with my mother. Although according to her, they never had sex. So, there's no question of whether I was his child or not, but he still wanted me to bear his name. I'm thankful for him in a lot of respects because again, in the early seventies, late sixties, it wasn't popular to take on a child that was not yours. He did that with no fear of child support or anything else. So, Benjamin Perry gave me something as valuable to me as my DNA, which was his name, Perry. I cherish my name. Thank you, Benjamin. He is my father.

Now, later on, I would have another father in Sherrell Evans, a stepfather, we'll get into that to that a little later, but I wanted to start off telling you about my mother. The woman she is and was. She is now deceased. We lost her about a year ago and she's my friend. She was 19 when I was born. She and I absolutely grew up together. Life is comprised of many moments and the moment that God gave me to her is an absolute defining moment in my life. She has influenced so many other moments that you'll get to see if you stay here with this book. My name is Rodney Perry and my mom is Venice Celeste Hunt Evans Coleman. I miss you, mommy.

CHAPTER TWO

Early Years

All right, so the original title for this book was going to be 100 Moments On My Journey. As I began to kind of think about the moments, I realized that I had far more than a hundred moments. So, I changed it to moments on my journey. So here we go, moment number one. Now I wanted to talk about my mother, mommy, but before I could talk about my mommy or my mother, I have to talk about Venice. An amazing woman and I imagine an amazing girl. When you hear people talk about her, they would mention how brash she was. She was a small woman, about five feet, three inches tall. Boisterous and larger than life. She's a fighter.

She's all those things. Her claim to fame was that she had a fight with Chaka Khan, the legendary Rhythm and Blues star. They went to high school together, Calumet High School, in Chicago, Illinois. My mother had a boyfriend, I forget what his name was. It kind of escapes me now, but Chaka Khan had an eye on him, so they ended up face to face in a vestibule and they got it on. When telling this story, Mommy would always make it clear that she wasn't fighting over "NO Man". She's say Chaka was disrespectful and the disrespect had to be dealt with. For years I did not believe this story. Fast forward many years later, I'm working on The Mo'Nique Show. Chaka Khan is the guest on the show and as we were shooting the show, my mother is in the front row. There was a moment when I saw Chaka see my mother and I saw fear come over this woman like I've never seen any other human being.

I was like, "Oh shit"! My mother beat up Chaka Khan! That describes my mother in a nutshell, the most loving, most caring, most brash fighter in the world. She taught me to love. She introduced me to Jesus, she taught me resilience, and she taught me not to be a follower. Most importantly, she taught me to be a leader and I miss her profoundly.

This book is comprised of countless moments; Benjamin Perry is my father, but I have many fathers'. Leo Jordan, my biological father. He was an older man he and my mother fell in love and I was the result of that union. Although the forbidden love, I, well I'm what you call an outside child. Leo was married with children when he got my mother pregnant. For many years my mother would tell me simply that she was in love with him. Conversely, towards the end of her life, she told me "he took advantage of me". He took advantage of her because he was grown. And in an era of the "Me Too" movement, I think it was a revelation for her, toward the end of her life. Nevertheless, God doesn't make mistakes and because of their forbidden love, you have Rodney Perry today, but I digress.

Benjamin Perry, this guy is impressive to me for a lot of reasons.

The main reason being that he gave me his name, knowing that I was not his biological son. According to my mother, they never had sex. So, there is no way he was mistaken.

He made a decision. He said this child is not going to be a bastard. He gave me one of the most valuable things. Leo Jordan gave me his DNA. Benjamin Perry gave me his name, for that I say, thank you. I say thank you for your name. I say, thank you for your family. I say, thank you for sharing that with me. I LOVE YOU MAN.

Mookie is my childhood neighborhood nickname. The irony of that nickname is this, my wife Angela Perry has the same childhood nickname. We were married five years before either one of us realized that. Mookie says several things to me. If you use Mookie, I know you're probably from the south side of Chicago. I know you probably grew up with me. I know you were either a family member or you're, someone from 77th and Bishop area.

That's Mookie. My grandmother calls me Mookie my uncle calls me Mookie my cousins call me Mookie. Mookie was a happy kid, always had a smile on his face. It was great to be Mookie. Mookie was friends with people like Killer, Bozo, and Faye. He had a great childhood.

Shorty. Now if Mookie was my childhood nickname, Shorty was my next nickname. Shorty was my nickname from let's say, ages eight until maybe 12 or 13. I grew up on 126th & State Chicago, Illinois. There was a guy Zack. Zack would give everybody their nickname. When I met Zack, he took one look at me and said wassup Shorty and that was it I was Shorty in our neighborhood until I grew a little bit. So, if you call me, shorty, I know you from 126th & State, or you are just tall as hell.

Terrance Terrell, Glenn Trammell were neighbors on my block. Just to think about this brings back so many memories. Shorty was the next evolution of Mookie. Mookie became Shorty. Shorty was cussing. I started cussing at seven years old. I mean some world-class cuss words. So, a shout out to Zach who gave me that nickname. I ain't short no mo'.

My best friend I talked about Venice now, I'm not talking about mommy, and that's what I called her Mommy! We were friends, we grew up together, and this lady was and is absolutely the most polarizing figure in my life. They called us the double mint twins because she took me everywhere. Wherever she went, she took me, and she would tell me stories. "Rodney when I had you, people were killing their children" She was always dramatic. but this was a fact. So, it was always remarkable that she even had me during that time, 1970, and instead of leaving me to be raised by my grandmother, which a lot of her peers did. She would take me with her; whether it was work, whether it was out to play cards with her friends, whether it was at tucks house or gene's house or wherever. We were inseparable. I suppose that is why I was really hard to lose her because not only was she my mommy, but she absolutely is and was my best friend.

Mammaw and Pawpaw my grandmother and my grandfather. Now, as I'm, going through the process of writing this book. I always felt like I was the product of a single parent home. I really had many fathers' and many men to contribute to who Rodney Perry would become. Now Pawpaw or Curtis Walton is my longest memory of a grandfather. He did all the grandfather stuff. He would take me to the store, he would buy me a sweater. He would, give me some candy and make me a sandwich. He was my paternal male influence. He was also an alcoholic. I think he used me to get out of the house to go buy his vodka. Hey, that's another story. What I saw with him and my grandmother was pure love. I can vividly remember them dancing and singing in the Living Room. "Baby sweet baby I didn't mean to run you away. You were the first on my list...". He was her "honey" and she was his "Poochie Woochie." It always felt like love. Their relationship is absolutely going to affect the rest of my life. I know that.

The young years, Ronnie and Uncle John. My mother had two siblings: Ronald and her older brother, John. Now John is named after my mother's father, John Hunt. If you've ever heard me do a joke about Junior, well Junior is Uncle John. The joke is basically about infidelity and mistakes and the woman in the joke has a child that is clearly not his child. Well, John Hunt my mothers' father was a fair-skinned man. My grandmother was a fair-skinned woman. Yet John Hunt Jr was a dark-skinned man. The scuttlebutt around the family is that there was a man that Mammaw dipped off with and that was John's Father.

My Uncle John was a remarkable guy. Although he spent some time in the crazy house. That's what they used to call it back then and that's where he met his wife, Judy, my white aunt, who would prove to be one of my most awesome aunts. This lady would give you a gift for every holiday. It was just incredible. Uncle John was my favorite uncle. No diss to Ronnie because Ronald Walton unquestionably makes me laugh more than any other human being in the world. My uncle Rahee is perhaps my first look at comedy. Now that I'm thinking about it, he is definitely the funniest Human I knew before I truly understood what comedy was.

John Hunt was my mother's father, a business owner, an entrepreneur. I'm sure that's where my entrepreneurial spirit came from, this man. He owned funeral homes, the golden state funeral homes, no black vehicles, all gold. I remember watching his whole court, he would sit outside the funeral home. He would pull his pants just above his knee to expose his sock his garters and the people that worked for him and his friends would sit there and listen and laugh as he would tell stories. Wait, I think my grandfather was a comedian! It all makes sense now. I have his body type too. He was a wealthy man for that time and that era. When you hear people talk, they always talk about how John Hunt helped their family because when you own a funeral home, you have to be where people are at their best and their worst times. I remember when we lost him, it'd been a very tough task for my mother. They were very close.

Sherrell Evans. If Leo Jordan is my biological father, Benjamin Perry gave me his name, Sherrell Evans gave me a lot of my man shit. He gave me shit that I don't and won't ever do and he gave me some stuff that I do, because of him. Let me explain. First of all, as a stepfather, he never made me feel as if I wasn't his child. I was there before his children came along. Well, his children with my mother anyway.

He would take care of me during the day. When there was an issue with a babysitter, he said, no I'll take care of him. I look back on that. He was a fairly young man. That was a lot to take on as a kid. I mean, I was under seven years old and what I learned from him was to be a provider. Sherrell Evans was a remarkable, provider. We had things. He led a pretty nefarious life. He was in the drug game.

One moment that sticks out in my mind was when Sherrell, we called him Shirl, and I got arrested. One of his friends had stayed the night with us while the entire city of Chicago was looking for him. Fortunately, by the time they tracked him to our basement apartment, he was gone. They still took us in. I remember asking him "what was going to happen to me?" He replied in his simplistic way... "you're with me… I got you". I never saw his friend again. From my mom's stories, he was a hired assassin.

Ultimately, they ended up letting us go. They probably let him go because of me. He never let anything like that touch our family again. I give him credit for that.

Punkin and Kiety, Rocky and Cedric. I have four cousins, two on my mom's side too. On Sherrell's side. The Evans family has always been awesome to me. I want to stop and acknowledge every member of the Evans family. I am their family and they are my family. Sometimes there is more than blood that ties us. Rocky and Cedric were brothers. Rocky taught me how to defend myself.

Cedric was both of our protectors; he would protect this little dude from way out south, from the real Chicago streets and he would have to protect Rocky from himself because Rocky would knock a motherfucker out without hesitation. To this day, if I need some help, I can call Rocky. These guys are not only my cousins, but they're also my brothers. Now equally on my mother's side of the family was Punkin and Kiety, Kevin and Keith Harris.

Their Grandmother and my Grandmother were sisters. I wasn't allowed to run the streets, but I could be social at Punkin and Kiety's house. My first parties were with them. Although Punkin and I were the same age, he was like a big brother to me. When you are the oldest child you feel alone. With these four guys, I was never alone.

CHAPTER THREE
Formative Years

Rodney Perry. I'm a professional comedian. I've been doing comedy at this point for over 30 years, but I've found comedy very early. I tell the story of having a teacher that in second grade would let me tell jokes at the end of the day if I would shut up throughout the course of the day. That teacher was Mr. Thompson. He suffered tons of ridicule from us kids. Oh my God. We were horrible to this guy. I mean, we would talk about this man and giggle behind his back. He had the wherewithal to have this little loud black kid to perform at the end of the school day. I would imitate Howard Cosell and Muhammad Ali. I found comedy before that because my parents would have get-togethers and they would listen to party records.

Richard Pryor, Moms Mabley, Bill Cosby. I mean five or six adults in the living room drinking, kicking it and smoking, listening to a record and laughing. My bedroom was right off of the living room so I would lay on the floor while they listened to the records and laugh. I was amazed by how the people on the records could captivate the room and they weren't there. When nobody was around, I'd get the record and go listen to it myself. "When I first came down here Jack", Richard Pryor, I knew every single word, Richard Pryor Live in Concert. I would become well versed in all things, Pryor. I searched for similarities between him and myself that probably didn't matter to anybody. By the way, did I mention that we share the same initials yep R.P.? I'm sitting in my office right now, writing this book and I am surrounded by Richard Pryor. A shadow box of Richard Pryor. The Richard Pryor box set and I'm looking at a t-shirt that I had made into a picture that I have on the wall as well. Richard Pryor absolutely changed my life.

If Richard Pryor is my grandfather in comedy, Eddie Murphy is my father. Pryor made me laugh but I never saw myself becoming what he was. Then there was Eddie Murphy. When I saw Eddie Murphy on Saturday Night Live, my life changed that day. I was spending the night with Punkin and Kiety where we would bowl Saturday morning and I would spend the night Saturday night. We watched Saturday Night Live and I saw Eddie Murphy do a character called Velvet Jones.

That moment would put my life on track because Pryor was very unattainable, but what Eddie Murphy was, I could see me being. He was dark in complexion, he was brash, he was cussing and he was cussing on network tv. Velvet Jones looked at the judge and said "but your honor; the bitch is ugly". It was like being struck by lightning. What? Can you say that on TV? I knew right there at that moment, that was me. That's what I wanted to be. That's who I wanted to be. Eddie Murphy, that Guy. Wow.

This moment is near and dear to my heart. Sheri is born. My sister Sherrell Evans. I remember it like it was yesterday. I was yearning for siblings and they granted my wish. The first child of the union between Sherell and Venice. Sheri's name is Sherrell Veniece Evans. I was a horrible big brother. I would tease her relentlessly. I would call her stupid under my breath. "You stupid". She would get so mad. The crazy part is she is probably actually the smartest person in our family, not stupid at all. My sister was known for her baby temper tantrums. She would cry and they'd say she was mean. While crying she would hold her breath until her face turned purple. Even today if she gets mad at your ass, she's mad at your ass almost forever. That's who she was and who she is.

As she got older, we became friends. She became my Saturday morning partner. We would get up, go sit on the couch, watch cartoons and eat cereal. We would play *I Declare War*, for hours on end. She's my little sister and I love her, and you bet' not say anything about her otherwise you have to deal with me.

126th and State 12-6 G D. The Gangster Disciples ran our neighborhood. I was lucky enough not to get involved in the gang life. It was an easy lure because if you lived in a Gangster Disciple neighborhood you were a GD by default. You see, I grew up on 126th and State Street, that part of Chicago is now known as the Wild Hundreds. Back then it was suburban America.

It was quiet, but it was definitely becoming "Wild". The street I lived on seemed so big to me. Recently, I went back for a visit and I realized it was just a little two-lane street. So many faces; Leonard Sago, Keith Terrell, the Black family. Every Halloween the big boys in the neighborhood would all turn on us and chase us for hours and we would have to hide from these dudes. I saw my first fine woman in that neighborhood. Her name was Janiece. She had a big old bootie. She lived across the street from Mr. Pippin, which I'll talk about in a little while. Then there were my friends, one block over on Brayton; Darryl Cole, Vicki, Brian Ross. We had a block club. It was nice, man. It was a great area. We had a home. I grew up in a house, One thing about Sherrell Evans, he was a good provider.

The block club had a trip to Orlando, Florida. That's the first time I got to go anywhere without my parents. It was great. We took a bus from Chicago to Orlando, Disney World. It's amazing to see the Magic Kingdom. I remember I was looking at Mickey like, "Yo, this is amazing". Oh my God, we were such little hood kids from Chicago. We weren't really like project kids, but we were definitely from the hood. We were all fish out of water in Orlando, Florida.

Money was sparse. So, we decided to steal. Ah, let me tell you something, if you're going to steal from anybody, don't steal from Mickey Mouse. The back end of Disney world is like another city. We were trying to steal some pencils or something. I only remember myself getting caught. They were threatening to me to put me in Mickey Mouse jail. One of the ladies from the block came and got me and assured me she's going to tell my mamma. I knew I was going to get my ass beat. I don't remember her telling my mother, but I also have never stolen anything else.

Alright, I did play baseball. I started playing baseball fairly early at about seven years old. I played for the White Sox. Roseland little league was instrumental in keeping you out of the gang life and giving you something to do. Our coach was Mr. Pippen. When I tell you this guy was all of our fathers, he was. John Smith (was the coolest kid of all time), Kay Kay (the guy who coined the phrase wild 100's), Brandon and Eddie Cole (Brandon became a comedian and filmmaker), Carl Seaton (a Hollywood producer and director now). From age 7 to almost 14 I played baseball. I could never hit. I didn't know until I was in the Navy that I needed glasses. I probably could have been a good baseball player if I'd had some damn glasses though. I've still got a scar on my face right now because I would always be playing, laughing and giggling. Playing third base at practice and took a hot shot right in my face. Roseland little league and Mr. Pippin were instrumental in forming who we would become as men, keeping us out of trouble. Thank you, Mr. Pippin! Love to you and your family.

Bishop is a place and a point in time. My grandmother has had a home on 77th and Bishop my entire life. We would often go visit. I had another set of friends over there. I had my neighborhood friends at home, but the Bishop boys we had fun.

People like Boz and Killer were my friends. I'm not sure why they called him Killer but I'm sure he wasn't one. Actually,

I was texting back and forth with Killer the other day. I would become friends with the whole neighborhood. There were a bunch of us around the same age, give or take two or three years. Whether it was Tim or Melvin, including the girls, there might've been 25 kids in that neighborhood. We would play football, basketball and foursquare. We had huge block parties. The neighborhood was so kinetic. Now it's quiet but it was amazing back then. Winter or Summer, we played football. We didn't have a field. We played on a strip of grass and concrete with a big rock in the center of the field. You would just have to make your way around the rock, avoid the car to get open. Between Bishop and State Street, Punkin and Kiety's crib and Cedric and Rocky's the streets of Chicago raised me.

Carver High School. I graduated from Gompers elementary school. Coming from Gompers you would either attend Julian, Corliss or Carver High School's. I'm not sure why I chose Carver. Maybe because Carver was the newest of the schools and it was really close to our home, but it was also located in the heart of Altgeld Gardens. The Gardens were the projects, but they weren't like the high-rise projects from *Good Times*.

So, my high school career was a bit uneventful until I got a burgundy Kangal for Christmas. I wore my Kangol to school and this gang banger tried to take it. Well, he took it, and so I was like "give me my Kangol back!" I snatched it back and we got into a scuffle. I punched him and the punch landed. Then I got scared. Dude whooped my ass. Whooped my ass and took my Kangol. As I've been putting together this book. I realize that I'm like, 0-3 in fights in my life and it's really disrespectful. I might pick a fight just to get a win next week. I might lose that too.

I would only be at Carver High School my freshman and sophomore years, but I still count that as my school. I learned some very valuable lessons at Carver High School. One thing most people don't know about me is that I can draw, well I could draw.

There was a guy in my art class, this guy was the most awesome artist I had ever seen up to that point in my life. He could draw an entire city. Because of him, I stopped drawing. I was like, "I'm never going to be that good". So, I stopped. As I look back, I realized how stupid of a decision that was. You can't base your art on how someone else does their art. I'm sure that's why I'm still a comic because I don't look at other people's art. I only look at my own art, and I don't judge my art.

Wow. That's a revelation. I don't judge my art based on other people because it's my art. Had I not stopped drawing because of that guy, I may not have learned this lesson. So, everything happens for a reason.

126th and State streets were wrought with gangsters. I remember at Gompers elementary school, some gang bangers coming up to me. They wanted me to become a gang member and I was like, "okay, but I gotta ask my mom", and I did. I asked my mother, could I join a gang? "Hey Mom, these guys want me to join their gang". She said "boy have you lost your damn mind? What are you a follower or a leader? You make a decision now and you let them know that you're already in a gang, My Gang. That was the lady I was dealing with.

CHAPTER FOUR
Things Change

So, I told you about Sherrell and him living the drug life, well us living the drug life. The thing about drugs is that you have access to them and eventually you will become a user. Their drug of choice was cocaine. Cocaine gave way to freebase. My parents Sherell and Venice were freebasing cocaine. The same thing that would burn up my idol Richard Pryor. I don't know if I understood it, but I understood it. If you're reading this and you have a child that you don't think gets it, they probably get it. I knew what it looked like. I knew what it smelled like. I don't indulge in drugs now because of it.

The drugs created a space where things began to change in our home. We had a pretty harmonious life. Even though Sherell was in the life, he never let that life touch us. My childhood, my siblings Childhood was a nice childhood. And the drugs, as I look back and reflect, the drugs were definitely a changing point. Cocaine.

Because when Sherrell was on cocaine, there was no peace in that house. He would literally say, "it ain't gonna be no peace in this house". I remember one Halloween, I was out hanging in the streets with my friends, you know, trick or treating or whatever. We got in some trouble and the police picked us up and they had to bring me home. I dreaded the police bringing me home because I knew that waiting at home was my mother and my step-father getting high. I didn't really want to be the one that would bring them down. A sad thing for a kid to have to think about. Drugs can definitely damage a home.

I was a sandlot football legend. Please believe that Rodney Perry was something else on the Outfield grass of Roseland little league. We played with all the cats from the Indian trails, Eric Mendenhall was their leader. Then there was all of us from 126th and state; Darrell Cole, Brian Ross and a bunch of others. It would be 20 guys out there, 10 on 10. When I tell you, I thought I was Walter Payton. I was the most elusive running back ever to touch a football. This is a fact. Then I went to Carver High School and started playing organized football. I quickly realized I knew nothing about football. I thought I knew football. They put me at defensive end by the way. I was a small guy my nickname was Shorty for God's Sake. One of the guys that we used to play with on the Sandlot was the quarterback, he ran every play to my side. Have you ever had your face step on? It's no fun.

House music. As I think of moments in my life, house music definitely affected my journey. There were three types of kids; the brainy nerds, the gang kids, and the party kids. I was smart but never brainy and I already told yall I was 0 and 3 in fights, plus my mother wouldn't tolerate the gang life so ... House music was it. If I hadn't gotten to the party world, I would have definitely become a gang member. So, thank you House music. Thank you, Frankie Knuckles and Steve Silk Hurley and all those great Chicago DJ's. Learning to DJ is still on my bucket list.

Eddie Murphy: Comedian. It's a through line in my comedy life. Eddie Murphy's first album. People are well versed with RAW and Delirious but Eddie Murphy, had an album before both of those called Eddie Murphy: Comedian. Brian Ross, Danny Nash and I would listen to this album every day. Every single day. We knew every single word. Early Rodney Perry was absolutely influenced by Mr. Murphy. Comedians don't really get to have influences. If you sound too much like the person you idolize you run the risk of having them despise you. Glad I didn't meet him until much later after I had found my own voice.

Circulating around the school were these phone numbers to sex lines. So, you would call a number and you'd hear, "hey, how are you? Yeah, I'm taking my clothes off". And it was like a recording or it might've been a real human, I don't remember.

We discovered this and we would call. The three-way call had just started. So, one person would call and a few of us would listen. We were giggling and laughing at one another, my dumb ass was making the calls. It hadn't occurred that maybe these calls weren't free. Mommy got that bill and whooped me like I was a slave like my name was Kunta. Kinte.

She kicked my ass but that wasn't the hard part. The tough part was facing my uncle. My uncle Ronnie ridiculed me to no end. He would call me and mimic the voice of the women from the 976 numbers. He was an asshole and I deserved all of his jokes.

I learned something about women watching my mother and my stepfather. Yes, Sherell was a great provider. I learned that being a great provider is not enough. I learned how strong my mother really was. She conquered her addiction and his abuse in a matter of a few weeks. She never went through a day of Rehab. Every time she wanted to do something, she just did it. She stopped doing drugs, just like that.

Our family had grown. Sheri, Ron, and JT had arrived. Sherrell had become very abusive. I'm talking about he would beat my mother with his fist. He beat her one time with a tennis shoe in her face and the tread from the tennis shoe was on her face. My mom would lose some of her hearing as a result of these beatings. I got to the point where I was done. I wasn't going to watch it another day I went out to our garage, he had a, a litany of tools. I grabbed a wrench probably about a foot long and I took it to my bedroom.

The next time he was sleeping, I was going to bash his skull in. I'm not a violent man. I'm not a violent person. I wasn't a violent boy, but I was prepared to kill this guy to stop the havoc he was unleashing on our family.

My mother found it. She found the wrench. "What are you going to do with that?" I said, "this is for him". She replied, "so what if he wakes up to kill you or what if you do kill him? Then what?" I think she made up her mind at that moment that we had to go. A lot of people will see an abusive situation and they'll ask, "Why didn't you leave?" Why do women stay? People stay for a number of reasons. We stayed as long as we did because Sherell was an excellent provider and there were things that we had that we may not have had without him. As a mother, I'm sure she wanted to afford us those things. So, we stayed until we weren't staying anymore. When I tell you it was abrupt! One day my mother showed up with a moving truck and just like that, we were headed to Monroe, Louisiana. We packed an entire house in a couple of hours. I don't know where he was. Maybe he was out of town. I'm not sure, but I know this, he came home to an empty house. We took everything leaving Chicago, man.

Leaving Chicago, it's something that I never had thought about. I mean, you know, I wasn't trying to leave Chicago. I'm in high school now. It was the summer, but I understood we had to go. I don't remember the drive down. As a matter of fact, I don't even think we drove. I think we flew. No, we took a train. We took a train south, I want to say to Jackson, Mississippi. We drove into Monroe from there. Monroe, Louisiana, it was a new world. I became a bulldog, Carrol High School. Monroe is a much smaller city than Chicago.

I might have been a bit arrogant. I was definitely a bit arrogant. You know I'm from Chicago. I had my little Chicago Swag. I had navigated Chicago and had managed to stay out of the gang life, but I knew what that was. You know, I was 0-3 in fights, but I was ready to do it again. I had my chance at organized football but with this fresh start, I was ready to do better, to leave my mark. I've always been a fast maker of friends, I hit the ground running. We got there in the summer, the Football team was already practicing, and the head coach was Lee Fobbs former NFL running back. My mom and Lee were friends, so it was a no brainer for me to get on the team. My mom said, "I'm going to talk to Lee, get you on that football team."

During that summer I made friends with my teammates so even though I was the new kid it didn't feel like that because I knew all of the players. I had been with these guys for two-a-days all summer. By the beginning of the fall, I was in the best shape of my life. I looked great. First of all, the high school in Chicago and the high school in Louisiana were two different things. Let's just look at the lunches; Chicago for lunch we might have gotten a big hunk of Bologna on Bread but in Monroe, Louisiana, there was soul food in the lunchroom. I mean baked macaroni and cheese, greens, fried chicken, red beans and rice and catfish on Friday. It was crazy.

The first back to school event was a sock-hop. It was amazing! I was fun and popular. I was the new kid, but I knew all of the right folks. I was on an emotional high. Headed home from the sock-hop riding my high, I had to cross a highway 165. There are a couple of different routes I could have taken home. This particular day, I went over the bridge. I had never gone this way before. If I would have been in Chicago, what was about to happen, would never have happened. This Chicago kid walked into the midst of at least five or six guys. The next thing I know, they just start swinging on me. They didn't want to steal anything. They just started kicking my ass. I flailed in order to get them up off me and I ran back down the steps of that bridge. They didn't chase me. I had gotten jumped.

As I'm thinking about it now, maybe it was disrespectful to pass through the center of those guys. They jumped me, bloodied up my face. I remember that run home tears streaming down my face.

What did I do?

What did I do to deserve that? Everything you go through in life is a lesson. You learn what you're made of. What type of resilience you have.

Carroll Bulldogs the blue and gold. I would be in Monroe at Carroll High School my junior and my senior year. I made some lifelong friends there. Some great human beings and everybody cared. Coming from Chicago where every student is a number, going to a historically black High School in Monroe, Louisiana, it just felt like a community. Most of these kids had been together from the first grade or kindergarten. They had a connection that I didn't have, but at the same time they welcomed me with open arms (except the six dudes that jumped me). I was a bulldog.

CHAPTER FIVE
Coming of Age

Now, Caroll high school was the spot. Our arch rival was Wossman High School. I would meet some lifelong friends in the halls of Carroll High School. Dietrich Mitchell and Michael Daniels let's start there. I don't remember how Deke and I met. I'm sure we met in some class that we shared. Dietrich took me under his wing. I've always been a bridge between people. If this group were my friends and this group were my friends, I was the bridge that made us all friends. The hood of Monroe is called Booker T. and they would be my tour guides through Booker T. So, Deke would take me everywhere. He had an El Camino that we would all pile in. Deke was grown. We were in high school, but Detrick Mitchell always seemed like a grown ass man to me. He was also always a ladies man. He knew how to talk to people. Even now, he's still the most charismatic guy in the room. You can't talk about Deke without talking about his mom. She would make me fudge if she knew I was coming by their house. When you become friends, you become a surrogate family member. Then there was Big Mike Train, Michael Daniels. The Daniel family was amazing, just good people. Mike's Dad was a pastor. He gave us a picture of what a real man looked like.

I couldn't write this book without including my friends Dietrich Mitchell and Mike Daniels, two of my closest friends. You can't have moments in my coming of age years without bringing up my man, Allen Fisher. Allen connected me to another group of guys. You've got Allen Fisher, you've got T. Harris, you've got Tut, and together we were 4 the hard way. If we could sing, we'd probably be a washed up R&B group by now. Allen drove a BMW in high school. I remember hanging out with him one day and coming home and telling my "Mama, I want a BMW." She responded, "What are you talking about boy?" She said "you don't have any idea what those people did to get that BMW. You don't know what price they had to pay." She was right. I would find out later that Alan and his family had lost their father to a railroad accident. And because of that, they've received a large settlement that allowed them to buy their home and some other things. I'm sure they would've given it all back to have another day with their father. You never know what people went through to get what they have.

I was 16 and in love with Kutanya Chapman. This might be the only time I've said it out loud or have written it anywhere. Kutanya Chapman was beautiful to me. I would be so nervous around her. I was scared to say anything. Maybe I wasn't her type. We are still friends. Yep, permanent friend zoned. It just never happened. The crazy part is while I'm typing this right now, I'm getting flustered. She was always nice and still a gorgeous girl. I dated this older girl. Her name escapes me. Ok, wait dated? That is a bit of a stretch. At best we were pen pals, but I was absolutely in love with her. She would mail me letters with perfume on them and I would write her poetry. Keep in mind, at this time I was still a virgin and I didn't lose my virginity till shit …18.

"You are the one of which my every thought is for
it is for you and only you I will long forevermore
by day I picture smiling as to jest
by night I picture you purring from my caress
each and every day I see you in another light.
First yellow then blue but never the dark of night
for you know as I do the picture I paint of you
is that of the one ever, ever so true."

That shit was smooth. Right? I would go on and say that poem to anybody that would listen.

Carla Hartwell is currently still in my life because we have a child together. I met Carla at the beginning of her freshman year which was the beginning of my senior year. All of the senior boys would prey on the unsuspecting new freshmen. Carla and I took to each other immediately. She and I were as hot at two teenagers could be. We would find anywhere to make out. Behind the curtains of the auditorium, empty classrooms, anywhere. She was sexy and fine as all get out. We carried on for almost that entire school year. I'm not sure why we broke up, but I'm sure we did. Then there was that faithful day; Carla came by our apartment to chat with me about us maybe getting back together. We went into the apartments' work out facility to have some privacy and proceeded to have some sex. Our baby, Hope Latasha Hartwell was conceived there. God Gave us the one person that would keep us both in line for years to come.

Octavia Turner, I was completely in Love with this young lady. Everything I had with my Pen Pal and everything I had with Carla combined. in the words of Eddie Murphy ", she stimulated my mind as well as my loins". I actually had to call Tay to recall how we met. She and I are still friends. We met at a night club in Monroe. I had already graduated high school and Allen, Tee, Tut and I would frequent Monroe's nightlife. We were kind of grown but not really. She was a student at Grambling State University, but she would come home frequently. I remember us being madly in love. When we made love, it was like you see in the movies perfect lighting and all. Young love at its finest. She would be the first woman I would see have an orgasm. To the ladies before her, my bad. It must not have been in God's plan for us to have a child because I don't remember us ever using protection. Octavia and I spoke recently and she reminded me that I proposed to her. I have no recollection of that at all, probably because she said no. After I got back from boot camp, I popped the question. She felt we were too young. Crazy how the mind protects your heart. We would grow apart after that and go off and live our respective lives. There is still a place in my heart for her.

You can't talk about Carroll high school without talking about our principal, Mr. Armen. He was a staunch disciplinarian, but he was also everybody's friend.

He made education his business and he and his staff truly cared about us. The difference between going to school in Chicago and going to school in Monroe is having a faculty that cared. Whether it was Mr. Rush that would regularly challenge you or Ms. Rambo who dared you to be better or Ms. Coats that taught us school could be fun. They were all constantly inspiring us, with love. These are the teachers that I remember but there was a litany of other teachers. Those educators absolutely formed the man writing this book today. So, to the teachers and faculty of Carroll High School CHS, love y'all.

I went to prom with this girl named Stephanie, a light-skinned girl with a Big Old booty. Oh, she was gorgeous. We were cool and we liked each other. I just didn't know how to really close the deal with her. She agreed to go to the prom with me. My grandfather owned funeral homes. He was known as the "Golden Boy", all his cars were gold. We went to prom in a gold limo. She wore a black and gold dress and I rocked a black tux with a gold cummerbund. I want to say we kissed that night and I remember her kissing me like, like an animal. If I was a better flyer dude, I'd probably have two kids with this girl. As it stands now, I can barely remember her name. Surely, I'm a blur in her past as well. Ultimately, I ended up in a friend zone with her. We just never did go beyond that.

Before we move out of high school, I've got to cover my football career. I was a sandlot legend, I told y'all that. I also played organized football in Chicago, but it got real when I joined the Caroll bulldogs. So, my junior year I was the bench warmer, you know, special teams' guy. I was determined my senior year to become a starting player on the squad. I worked hard. I got in the weight rooms, I bulked up, I put on about 15 pounds. I was a specimen. Now the only drawback to Rodney Perry the football player is that I was never fast. At my best, I ran like a 4.7 40-yard dash. We had some bonified speedsters. Both Mark Foy and Tony Hubbard ran 4.0 40-yard dashes. At any rate, I was a good fullback. I could block and I was intelligent. So, there are two full backs. Rodney Perry and this other dude. He was a big guy, 6 foot, all muscle.

He wasn't the sharpest knife in the drawer. Meanwhile, Rodney Perry is damn near genius! I'm breaking down the plays, I know what's going on. He should have gotten the job, but he never would get low enough when he ran. So, even though he was big and could run over people, he would be running up so high and they would take him down every time. It came down to the blue and gold scrimmage game to decide who would get the spot. I got the call, a 32 TRAP. I did my jab step got the ball and was out! No one touched me till I saw the safety. The job was mine. My life was about to change. I'm about to be the big man on campus. So first play of the season I was the starting full back, but I was still on the kickoff team. I ran down the field and one of my teammates got thrown into me, knee to knee contact. Just like that my football career was over. I'm out for the season., the most traumatizing moment of my life at that point. I cried like a baby not because of the pain because of the work I put in to get there and all of a sudden, I wasn't there.

I worked tirelessly after that injury to get back. I wouldn't make it back for the football season, but I did make it back for the track season. Again, I wasn't a sprinter, but I did run the mile and the two-mile because my endurance was crazy. That year I represented Carroll high school in the Louisiana state track and field meet running the mile and the 2 mile. Our track coach was

Warren Trimble. The absolute best motivator you want as a prep athlete is Warren Trimble. I can still hear his voice now. Whenever I think about quitting, I hear Coach Trimble saying "DON'T YOU QUIT ON ME SON!"

CHAPTER SIX
I Am a Man Now

About to embark on real life. Of course, I know now that is a very daunting task for a young man, especially a young black man in America. I had taken the ASVAB test on a whim one day to get out of class, and scored fairly well across the board, for every branch of the military. I was a pretty well sought after candidate for the military. The first recruiter that came calling was the army recruiter. I remember him being a squared away guy and a pretty straight forward and I must've been his first candidate because this guy pulled out all the stops for me. I mean, he was really on me taking me out to dinners and such. I felt like I was being recruited for college. We were virtually inseparable until I hurt my knee playing football. I hurt my knee and the look on his face said, dammit, lost one. I remember also a marine recruiter who hadn't really recruited me at all. But after I got hurt, he came and stood over my couch and was like, we got doctors they could fix that. I immediately told him to get the hell out of my house. Yeah, no, I'm good. Y'all crazy.

So now it's time to graduate high school, time to start living real life. I definitely had the comedy bug and I felt like I needed to go back to Chicago. I talked to my mom and she was like, cool, go stay with your grandma, and I did.

They welcomed me with open arms, but that got old quickly. If you live with anyone where you're not paying bills as a grown-up, you will become a burden very fast. Then came the questions. "So, what are you planning to do? What are your plans? Are you working? Are you going to work?"

All I knew was, I wanted to be a comedian. But this is the crazy part, I didn't know how to be a comedian. I mean, I didn't know any of the things I know now. I didn't know to go to the open mics. I didn't know to meet other comedians. I didn't know how to go about it. That's the big dilemma for most people with dreams, just you just don't know the process. I had no clue about the process. All I knew is that I wanted to make people laugh. That was eating away at my heart and my soul.

So, I'm sitting in my grandmother's house, 7757 South Bishop, Chicago, Illinois. Listening to the radio and I heard an advertisement, Robin Harris at the Regal Theater tonight. "Oh my God!" Robin Harris, Chicago comedy legend. I'm going. I didn't think to have a ticket. I was just going to go, and I did. I took the bus down 79th street to the Regal Theater and got off the bus and stood outside the Regal Theater. I heard this man dismantling the audience. I mean, I heard his muffled voice then an explosion of laughter, his muffled voice then explosion of laughter. I stood out there for about 30 minutes, I listened.

Then I got back on the bus and rode home on an emotional high. I had just, kind of had a brush with Robin Harris. I would find out that the following day, that was his last performance. I would later meet his wife and people that knew him closely and they would tell me that I bore some comparison to him. I can only hope as a comedian my last night on stage will be that epic. Rest in peace. Mr. Harris.

So, I go back to Monroe, Louisiana. Chicago wasn't working. I didn't know how to be a comedian. I didn't have any prospects for jobs. So, I went back home. I went back to Mama's house. I was working at Walmart then, I believe. I actually opened Walmart store number 1193. One morning, I'm at home chilling, I didn't have to be at work until that afternoon. My mom who was working at OIC (Opportunities Industrial Corporation), it was a nonprofit to help people find jobs and such. My mom was working there, and she hit me up, you know, let's say 10:00 AM "Hey Rodney, I need to borrow $20." I replied, "Well, no problem. Whatever you need." She called me a few minutes later. "You know what, I need $50." I said, "Ok, no problem", she called again ... "I need a hundred ". I responded "$100 Why? This little lady, my best friend, and the lady I know and love, cussed me out. "You ungrateful motherfucker. How dare you ask me why?" And I'm paraphrasing. She let me have it. She was upset. I was upset. You know what? "Keep your fucking money, be out of my house. Don't be there when I get there." So, guess what? I left, packed up my little stuff and I left. I went to stay at my buddy Larry's house.

His family welcomed me. His mom was a single parent. They had an extra bunk bed. I'm not sure if she reached out to my mom or not, but as a parent, I would have. I was there a few days when Larry comes to me. He says, "hey man, my mom said if you want to stay here, you gotta pay rent." I ain't got no damn rent money for yall if I'm going to pay rent I might as well pay my mama rent.

So just like that, I went back home with my tail tucked between my legs. My mother welcomed me. We apologized to each other. We hugged and kissed. That may be the only time my mother and I actually fell out. Now what we did learn over time is that we could not live together. I mean, we tried it a few different times in life, but you know, us living together, was always a daunting task.

Northeast Louisiana University NLU, it's no longer NLU. Actually, now it's ULM - the University of Louisiana at Monroe. NLU was great. It was not high school. It was college. College wasn't hard though, but I was taking some bullshit classes. I mean I took bowling for God's sakes. I knew I wanted to be in entertainment, so I took radio, TV, film, that was my major. I was at NLU maybe a year and a half. And those were great times. Still running with my boy Allen Fisher. You know, we stalked the campus looking for girls and from time to time we would meet a few. We had good times. Some great moments. I had my first drink on that campus. I didn't really drink in high school. Some of my peers drank alcohol. I didn't have a desire for that. In college, you would do whatever the girls wanted to do. We would buy this peach schnapps and orange juice to make fuzzy navels. We would get on it, dog gon it, off that peach schnapps. Allen and I would visit girls in their dorm rooms, talk to them and try to hit, or hit, that was our life.

A lot of people don't know that I actually started stand up in Monroe, Louisiana. There was a guy on a campus of NLU that was a comedian. I never met him face to face. He was like a celebrity. He hosted everything. I remember wanting to talk to him, but he might as well have been Eddie Murphy. He was untouchable. Plus, he was an upperclassman so there would be no reason for him to talk to little old me. Which is probably why I make myself available to any comedian that wants to chat now.

My very first performance, like a real standup comedy performance was at the nursing building at NLU. My friend Belvia was a nursing student and Bel was like Rodney, "we got this event coming up. I want you to be in it." I remember going up and doing that show and I remember smashing.

If I go back and stand there in the audience, maybe I was just okay. But in my mind's eye I see people laughing, big laughs. I was still a shell of what the big comic on campus was, but I was doing comedy.

I worked at Walmart. It was an amazing place. The Walmart Corporation is different since Sam Walton passed away. I worked in the household chemicals and when you work at Walmart, you become friends with your fellow associates. One of my friends worked in jewelry her name was Sonya, I believe, a pretty girl I would stop at the jewelry counter and crack jokes. She and I were like brother and sister because she was clearly out of my league. She had this thick little fine thang working for her. I would run a game on this girl and she would listen. So, one night after work me and that fine thang went by Sonya's crib to kick it. I looked this young woman in her eyes and said what I thought was the coldest lines a brother ever said... "Hey look, I like you but I'm just looking for something physical, can you deal with that?". She said yes and we made love on Sonya's floor behind her couch to the light of her stereo while Keith Sweat played in the background. When I tell you she dropped some world class vagina on your boy. I mean, my God, I remember eating my words. I was like "Yo, I know I said I just wanted us to be physical, but I have reconsidered, I think we should be together." She immediately replied, "Nah, I'm good. You said you wanted a physical thing and that's what it's going to be. We can continue this physical relationship, but we don't need to be together." The rude awakening. Dammit.

I'm a dad now. My relationship with Carla Hartwell had yielded a beautiful baby girl. Hope Latasha Hartwell. I remember standing across the bed from Carla's mom. Hope had been born safely. We were, standing there basking in the glow of having a new baby in our respective families and Carlas' mom looked across and said to me "so you're going to marry my daughter?". I quickly said, "No, ma'am." What type of guy says no ma'am? I didn't even try to lie. Carla and I have a pretty good relationship, not very adversarial. She's done an amazing job with our daughter. She never put me on child support and that in itself is remarkable. She's always been an entrepreneur. I'm an entrepreneur. I'm blessed. No, I'm lucky to have had a child with her and that child is amazing. If I have any regrets in life, it's not being there for Hope's formative years. I wanted to provide for her, but I didn't understand then that being there is more important.

Hope Latasha Hartwell is the best of both Carla and I. She is smart. She knows her books. She knows how to navigate the streets. She's funny. She's all those things and she's my firstborn. She made me a man. She made me step up and become the man that I needed to be. The first step in being a man is diapers. Carla would call me, right? "I need some diapers." I didn't have a car. I would walk to pick up the diapers then deliver them to Carla and Hope across town. On the way back I would stop at Michael Daniel's house and we would talk, hang out, and play dominoes or something until it was time for me to head back home. I had little stops along the way. Monroe is not a big town but I could get clean across it in 20 minutes on foot. I would call Mike from pay phones along the way. "I'm at Walmart." Click. Mike's mom always remembers that because she always says, "you were a good dad." Don't get me wrong, I'm not painting myself as the perfect father. I made some mistakes and some bad decisions as a young dad. We were probably way too young to be parents. One of the great things about God is he will bless you despite yourself. Because of my sense of responsibility for this child, I had to grow up and grow up fast.

While I was working at Walmart I found a better job that paid a little more money at a place called Shoe Town. It was a little closer to home too. Shoe Town was cool because not only would you get your pay, but you would get a little bonus based on your performance, so if you sold a pair of shoes, that was one thing. But if you sold some shoes and a sock, you'd get a little bonus just like that. I was good at it, talking to people, kicking it, having a good day. I was amazing at this job.

We lived on North 18th. I would walk to work. Summers in Monroe, Louisiana are nothing short of hot as hell. On this particular day I'm walking to work and a white car pulls up alongside me. Normally I don't take rides from strangers but it was hot. The guy could have been an ax murderer or a kidnapper.

As long as he had an air conditioner, I didn't care. I needed to be out of the elements. That gentleman was a Navy recruiter. If you know recruiters they're well versed in the art of the big sale.

I'm sure I wasn't a tough sell. I had already contemplated the military in high school. I had been out of High School a year and a half now. I was working and going to College.

I was a young father and it occurred to me that my mother was taking care of me and mine. She had her own children, my brothers and sister. It was time for me to go.

The recruiter on that ride pitched me the Navy. "I can get you money for school. I'd get you this and get you that." I said "you know what, sign me up." I was gone maybe a week later, headed to San Diego to boot camp. The Navy would change my life or maybe the Navy put me on track. Life is all about perspective.

CHAPTER SEVEN
The Navy

Military Enrollment Processing Station MEPS. Once you meet your recruiter, the recruiter tests you. You go through the MEPS for your physical and they test your aptitude and then you choose your job. I went to the MEPS a day early so I would be processed the following morning. That night, I'd meet Chris Rock. Chris Rock was touring with Heavy D. I believe they are related. I remember walking up to him, excited, you are Chris Rock? He said, "Yes, I am." I said, "Man, I'm a comedian too. Put me on. I'm about to join the Navy." He said, "I'm not even on myself." Then he disappeared into the night. I went through processing the next day.

I put comedy on the back burners as I became a member of the United States Navy. While I was being processed, I had to choose my job. My recruiter was a regular Navy recruiter, but I ended up picking something called the TAR Program: Training and Administration of Reservists. So, I inadvertently transitioned into the TAR Navy. It doesn't exist anymore. The TAR Program mobilized all of the Naval Reservists for Operation Desert Storm/Shield.

I was off to San Diego for boot camp. Boot camp is designed to change you from a civilian. A person that walked around and acted and reacted like an individual to a person that operated as a member of an organization, a team member. Your individual ways were over. You will walk with a group of 90 people in unison everywhere. To some of my shipmates' boot camp was like jail to others, it was fun.

Boot camp was interesting. They would challenge your fears. There were 90 guys in my company from all across the country. We all went through the same thing. The day came when we were to swim. It had never occurred to me that I was joining the Navy and that I might have to swim one day. Well, I couldn't swim. So out of the 90 guys in our company, maybe 10% of those people were African American. Nine of us all failed the swim test. Six of the guys wouldn't jump at all. So, the swim test goes as follows. You jump in 12 feet of water, you tread water, then you swim to the end of the pool and get out of the pool under your own power. If you can't swim, that's going to be pretty difficult. All of the black guys from the inner city couldn't swim.

Failing the swim test immediately boots you over to remedial swimming. A little more attention and you should pass at the very least. You should learn how to tread water and lift yourself out of a pool. I went through that. I had been there for about a week. If I didn't pass that last day, I would have to start boot camp over with another company. I remember that day vividly. The Navy Seals were there and they were helping us train. I was in the water and I was going under and this Seal, a big guy, black guy, glasses, Navy swim shorts. As I was going under, I heard him say, "If you die, I'll kill you." I quickly began to tread water, swam to the edge of the pool and pulled myself out. I can't thank that guy enough for my Navy career and scaring me out of that pool.

Most people come to boot camp knowing where they're going afterwards. I didn't, I went in what they called undesignated. So, I was scheduled to go to boot camp and go out to the fleet undesignated. I didn't understand what that meant then, but it wasn't a great deal. I volunteered to be the Yeoman of the company. There were company officers, a leading petty officer, a second in command and, and the Yeoman, who was in charge of carrying a box with all of our daily paperwork. Not only did he carry the box, but he would lead the march. The Yeoman was very important. It was a job that I both loved and cherished. I liked being a Yeoman so much that when I got an opportunity, I chose that for my job in the Navy.

I ended up being in the top 10% of my boot camp company. Even though I had shined in boot camp I was still undesignated. The next step for an undesignated sailor was apprenticeship training. There you would be prepared for fleet life.

I completed apprenticeship training at the top of my class. I was granted an opportunity to choose an A school. I had enjoyed being the Yeoman of my boot camp company plus I heard Yeoman always work in an air-conditioned office, so it was easy, I chose Yeoman A-School. Next stop, Meridian Mississippi.

A Yeoman is basically a secretary. I would learn the skills that I still use: typing, filing, learning computers, learning decorum and how to deal with people are some of the skills that I learned in that A-School. Also, there in Meridian, Mississippi, I met one of my lifelong friends. His name is Roy Freeman. Freeman and I only brushed in A School but we would end up at our first duty station together. I count him as one of my best friends now, Roy Dean Freeman, "Really Dick'n Freaks". He was a tall slim guy 6'3" 205 pounds. A good guy from McGehee, Arkansas. We ran the New Orleans streets with reckless abandon.

My first duty station was in New Orleans, Louisiana. Of all the places in the world to send a young man, New Orleans. "Oh my God!" If you can't meet a girl in New Orleans, you don't want to meet a girl.

We were all college age, but we had cars and money. We worked every day. New Orleans is a great city for anybody college age. You had several colleges. Xavier University, Southern University at New Orleans and Tulane just to name a few. So many colleges, so many girls. Great place to be a kid and be grown at the same.

I arrived in New Orleans. I would be working for Admiral Breshnahan maybe 21 years old and ready to be the best sailor I could possibly be. I remember my friend in my office, a civilian lady by the name of Delorah Green. Ms. Green would show me the practical way to use the skills that I learned in school. I was in charge of typing awards and answering congressional letters. I learned how important it is to simply write a letter when someone writes their congressmen. That letter is dispatched to any number of places that can actually address the concerns outlined in the letter. Our admiral would address certain things and I would draw up that correspondence. I learned a lot of valuable lessons in New Orleans.

My first day there hanging out with some older guys, they got me drunk. They gave me Whiskey ... "Old Grand Daddy" or something like that. I threw up like I had never thrown up before.

Moments On My Journey — Rodney Perry

Even though I was in the Navy, comedy was still on my mind. I found a gong show close to where I lived. "A gong show shouldn't be that bad". I went and I performed what I thought was some funny material. I got gonged. Somebody stood up, grabbed the stick and gonged me. Oh, it was horrible. I was shell shocked. I didn't leave right away, and I remember someone saying, "What are you still doing here? Didn't we gong you?" I remember thinking to myself, maybe this comedy thing ain't for me. This is some bullshit. I quit. I quit doing comedy. About two days later I was in the barracks. Some other guys were playing dominoes and there was a guy at the table, he looked like he was part Asian or Asian and black mixed, and he was playing dominoes with another guy, a marine, and the guy was talking trash.

His name was Harry, he looked across at the marine and said "boy if I was yo dentist ... I'd put a cherry bomb in your mouth and say, fuck it." The place erupted with laughter. I was like, whoa, that was funny. I went and pulled him to the side. I was like, "man, you are funny. You should be a comedian." He said, "A comedian?" I said, "Yeah, I used to do Comedy." I don't think he knew I had quit just days before meeting him. He looked at me like I was crazy. He told me "I'll do comedy if we can do it together", and we did just that. We became a comedy team, Ratch and Rod comedy explosion.

Thank God for Harry getting me back in comedy because if I don't meet that guy at that moment, maybe I don't become a comedian. So, we were Ratch and Rod. Harry Ratchford, Rodney Perry. We were roommates in the barracks, so we would make up jokes during the day and go do them that night. We booked our first gig. We got $176.58 and that was a check. We were so blue. Blue means we were cursing a lot. Oh my God. We had some crazy bits. We created a bit that was called, Donnels' Dick Emporium. On the heels of Loraina Bobbit dismembering John Wayne Bobbit, we thought you should be able to remove your member or maybe even replace it. We did that joke. Those older sailors and soldiers looked at us like, who booked these two dudes? They reluctantly paid us. It was our first check. We have both went on to buy homes, put children through college, all on comedy. All on jokes. Harry remains my best friend. Can't thank the Navy enough for giving me this guy.

On the weekends in New Orleans, we would go down to the Lakefront. The Lake Front on a Sunday is where everybody would hang out. You would take your car down there, clean it up. Cruise the lake and holla at girls. One particular day, I'm on the Lakefront. Me and my boys, I think I was riding with Freeman and I met this young lady. Every relationship starts with a hello. She was good looking, you know, she was sexy. Her name was Judy. She was a bit older than I was. We exchanged numbers on the Lake Front and started a relationship. We became physical fairly quickly. When you do grown stuff, grown things happen. Next thing I know I got the call Judy said she was pregnant.

Now there was a scam going around New Orleans. Girls would fake being pregnant to get the abortion money. Judy wasn't faking. She was pregnant for sure. I don't remember her being pregnant. Probably because I was scared shitless, I was already a father. I thought if I ignored the fact that she was pregnant the reality would just go away. I had even convinced myself that this child might not be mine. She called me to come over and meet my son. She wanted to name him Rodney. I wish I had done that. There was another guy around during that time, he's gone now. His name was Joe Bowns. Joe was from Chicago, I've always had people to protect me for whatever reason. People just want to make sure I'm okay. Joe was my protector. One day I was shooting dice in the barracks and lost my entire check. Joe came in and noticed the sadness on my face. He pulled me to the side and asked how much I'd lost. I replied, "My whole check." He said, "If you had more money could you win it back?" Like any good gambler, I said yes. Joe put the money in my hand and I went to work with new energy and new luck. As soon as I achieved my monetary goal, Joe said, "Let's go." Typically, you can't just leave a dice game but when Joe said it was over, it was over and nobody questioned it.

Joe would knock somebody out on my behalf. This guy would really protect me. We had so many great laughs. I miss my friend. So, when Judy delivered our child, I took Joe with me. Not a DNA test, Joe. Joe and I went into Judy's house. Joe took one look at that baby said, "boy, you better shut up that baby is yours man." I said, "Look at all that hair!" He didn't look like me to me. I'm also the dude that didn't think his biological father looked like him either. Joe said, "Forget that hair. Look at them damn feet." He was right. Judy and I have had our ups and downs. I can never be mad at her for real because she gave me my only son. Devin Devante Harris.

CHAPTER EIGHT
The Bay Area

Devin Devante Harris. My only son. His mom Judy was obviously a fan of JODECI, hence the middle name, Devante. My first two children Hope and Devin. I hadn't chosen their names. As I look back on my life, I would like to have named Devin after me but I'm glad I didn't because Devin is Devin, he's an individual. He doesn't have to be little Rodney or Rodney number two or Rodney the second. He's his own man. I think there are no mistakes in life. Devin is absolutely my heart. Harry used to call him mushroom because he had a giant afro, wide eyed and a happy face. Once I got past the fact that Devin was mine, fatherhood came easy to me.

Judy already had three children or four maybe, so she was very comfortable with me taking Devin. I would pick him up all the time. He rarely cried when he was a baby. I remember when I took him to meet my mom for the first time, she immediately fell in love with him. He was a great addition to our family. I believe that Devin is somehow spiritually connected to the world. I remember one moment I was going to visit a psychic palm reader and as I approached the door, I changed my mind. Devin was with me, and he pulled at me like dad. Go ahead, go in. To be honest, he really didn't even have a lot of words, but I knew what he meant. Even though we had just had a child our relationship was fading. I began dating this girl named Seandra. Seandra and I became friendly toward the end of her career at Xavier University.

We had spent the night together and I would never see her again. We said our goodbyes. I got in the car, a purple maximum. Freeman was driving but it was Malcolm's car. I was a scrub. Actually, I was a double scrub. I was riding on the passenger side of the car and it didn't belong to either one of us. This young girl walked in front of the car, wearing some little denim shorts with a big old booty. I flagged her down just moments after I dropped off Seandra. I flagged this girl down and we began to talk. She gave me her number. We've been talking for the past 22 years. Angela East would become my wife and mother of 4 beautiful girls. We would walk this journey hand in hand. Meeting Angela, absolutely put my life on track. Angela and I were inseparable. She had an uncanny knack for getting on base without me. She was not in the military, but she was just so resilient. We had spent probably a year or so together, my time in New Orleans was coming to an end and I had to make some decisions. New Orleans is a military town, so people weren't unfamiliar with Navy guys and marine guys coming into town and then leaving children and girlfriend and the wake.

I told Angela I was leaving, but I wanted her to come with me. I was going to come back and get her. I was headed to California now. Harry had already left for California and I began to try to get west to ultimately get to Hollywood. I would speak to my Navy detailer and he said, I have orders in the Bay Area. I looked at the map. The Bay was only a couple of inches away from Los Angeles. As you can see, I am and was geographically challenged. The Bay area was actually a six-hour drive from LA. Taking those orders to Oakland and San Francisco would prove to be the best decision in my comedy life. Daniel Dugar, Luenell, John Alston, Tony Royster, Rodney Perry, Harry Ratchford, Joey Wells, Katt N' Da Hat, just to name a few. There were so many of us in that comedy incubator at that moment. We trying to be funny and trying to figure out comedy, at the same time. There were so many great comedians in the Bay Area. I got to the Bay and before I even reported to my Navy job, I reported to comedy. Harry had been there for a month or so and hadn't been on stage. I couldn't believe it. I told Harry; "we are going up tonight."

I checked the newspaper, I called some people and I found a stage. The place was called the End Zone. The End Zone was owned by former Raider Clem Daniels. The people that populated the End Zone, were the most awesome, scariest people in the world. You can easily be sitting at a table with a dude that was up for murder, but they, like most people needed to laugh. Me, Harry, Joey, Mondale, Dugar and Luenell were all tasked with making these people laugh.

Harry and I got to the End Zone early. There was a flyer with Mondale on it. I told Harry, "That guy is famous. He's been on Def Jam." Actually, Mondale hadn't been on Def Jam, yet. I was wrong but I'm wrong a lot. The man running the room was a guy named, Rick Sullivan. A big guy with a raspy voice. The stage was in the corner of the room and I could not wait to get on it. I went up to Rick Sullivan and said "I'm Rodney, this is Harry. We want to get up tonight". He said, "well, I don't have room for both of you, but one of you guys can get up". I looked at Harry. I said, "Harry, you go." Harry said, "no, you go". I said, okay. Harry always reminds me that I was supposed to send it back to him but I didn't. I needed to be on that stage. The End Zone would become our comedy home. Every Tuesday night we would crack jokes, do competitions and play dominoes with Marv the manager of the End Zone. DJ dollar bill would provide the music that was the soundtrack of the End Zone days. It was a small place, maybe held one hundred people. That was a great time. We were young, telling jokes and we loved it.

Every comedian has another comedian that is tasked with giving them the game. That guy for me was a man named John Alston aka the Guru. John had had some brushes with major success and for whatever reason, it hadn't worked out but we had him at our disposal. John and I became friends. I would visit his home. I would be there when his son was born. We were fast friends. I consider him a friend even now, but we haven't talked in years.

John would share stories about comedy, what it was to be a comedian, how to do it the right way. John was fun and well written. He had the best of the comedy riff and great material. The jewels of comedy wisdom John dropped, helped me tremendously. The End Zone was our Oakland home, but the Punchline was our San Francisco home. Sunday nights at the punchline was awesome. You would see comedians like David Allen Moss. This guy was easily the best comedian I ever have seen. He was like watching Richard Pryor in his prime, but what I understood, he had moments where he was that guy but drugs and alcohol got the best of him. You see back in the day, from what I understand they used to pay him in drugs.

The punchline was an amazing spot. We would be there and after the show ended, we would all help put the chairs up and after that, they would open a bar. It became a social setting. Comedians talking comedy and drinking alcohol. There's nothing better. You can't talk about the End Zone and the Punchline without talking about Geoffrey's Inner Circle. Mister Geoffrey Pete owned the club downtown Oakland. The End Zone was grimy, the trenches. But if you got to play Geoffrey, that was the big leagues.

Geoffery's was run by a lady named Rose Gettis. A really pretty slim lady that was elegant and because of her, Geoffery's was an elegant stage with red velour curtains and a classy neon sign. If you worked there you were a part of the Bay Area comedy elite. Geoffery's didn't do shows every week. When they did, it was always a big deal. If you told folks that you were going to be at Geoffery's they would immediately look at you as if to say… "Oh, you're a real comedian?"

I had been in the Bay area for a few months. Angela and I continued to correspond but she was starting to not believe that I was going to send for her. Harry and I had an apartment in Fremont, California. We were wild for a minute, but I began to long for my girl and I wanted to keep my word to her. I sent for Angela. She joined me in the bay area. Well, hold it … to say I sent for her implies that I flew her out, nope I went to get her. She left the comfort of her home in Louisiana to travel across country. She and I drove from Louisiana to the Bay Area. The best test of any relationship is a car ride across the country. If you can make it across Texas with a person, you can make it through life with them. I was the first one to have a woman to join us in our bachelor pad. I had never lived alone, and I still haven't lived alone. Angela and I were young and in love. We were meant to be, so we were.

CHAPTER NINE
Crossroads

Yep. We were in Fremont, California. Angela joined me and Harry had a lot going on as well. Before we knew it, we had kids and everything. Our first stop was Alicante apartments, vaulted ceilings, wrap around balcony, an Olympic pool. We soon realized that we couldn't really afford Alicante, so we moved to Hayward, California to a place called Fletcher Towers. If Alicante was the "Jefferson's", then Fletcher Towers, was definitely "Good Times" and we did have some good times.

Harry, Makita, Angela and I all lived under the same roof. It was great, at first. Harry and I always did and still do get along. We were thick as thieves, but Angela, Makita not so much. Angie and I made it work co-habitating, sleeping in the same bed, living together, and paying bills. Before we knew it, we had a baby on the way. Our first child, Rachelle Hannah Perry. I was so happy to get an opportunity to be a father again. I already had Hope and Devin but it was going to be different with Rachelle. I was going to stay with this woman.

Angela and I began to have conversations about marriage. We decided we would get a marriage license. Before you get married, you have to get a marriage license. So, we did. What I didn't know at the time is that the marriage license, if not executed within a certain time period, will expire. So, I looked up one day as I was checking the license and I realized it was about to expire.

Angela and I had had been through the fire and she proven to me that she had my back. I woke up that morning, I said, Angela, "let's get married."

She said, "Okay." We went to the justice of the peace. We didn't spend $1 million dollars. We didn't spend $1 thousand dollars. All we had was each other. All we had was love.

The thing about getting married at the justice of the peace is that he has other things on his docket that day. Petty criminals, traffic tickets. Oh yeah. And marry these two young people. His name was Judge Jerome Nadler. After a full docket of crime he brought us into his chambers. Then he married us. I remember his name because I thought it was a black name and he was clearly a white man. He asked were we sure about what we're embarking on? We both said yes. Angela laughed uncontrollably during the ceremony. Still, don't get that. We're married now marriage is different than dating or going together. Marriage is ownership. My wife, my husband, we belong to each other now. We were both in uncharted waters. She was a product of a single parent and so was I. We would find out later that we were both outside children, which means our fathers had engaged in extramarital affairs and we were the products of that union. How ironic.

Angela proved to be a sober his voice in my life. She feels like I never take her advice, but I kind of always take her advice. I may not move when she thinks I should move, but her advice is always dead on. Whether it's about people or business. She doesn't care about nuance. She doesn't care if it's going to hurt people's feelings. She's just honest that's one of the things I love about her.

I was a comedian at night and a sailor during the day. I was like a superhero, but not really. I worked at, Moffett Field, a Navy man. I did my Yeoman duties during the day and at night I would crack jokes. Oakland, San Francisco, San Jose, and Sacramento: if you had a stage, I was on it. I was quickly becoming one of the most sought-after comics in the bay area. Our comedy community was amazing. Katt Williams, Joey Wells, Daniel Dugar, Luenell, Rip the Player, Comedy Dijon, Bubba, Will Walls, Glamis, Tess, Mondale, John Alston. This is just a few of the great comedians that were around. The Bay area comedy scene was dope. It could not be denied.

My tour in the Bay area was my second Navy tour. I was approaching eight years. That was a crossroad. They were starting to ask me if I was going to reenlist and I felt like if I were to re-enlist for four more years, that would take me to 12 years and a person that does 12 years in the military should go ahead and do 20. I knew I wasn't going to do 20, so it was time for me to go. I didn't have a conversation with Angela. I didn't talk about it with anybody, but my mom. I had made up my mind. I was like, "mom, I'm about to move to LA and pursue my comedy career."

She read me the riot act. "Who's going to take care of your children? I can't afford it." She gave me a hundred reasons why I shouldn't go forward. "The security of the military, the money: you need that Rodney, we don't even know if you're that funny." I'm talking about at least an hour. She gave me every possible scenario as to why I shouldn't move forward with this idea of leaving the military.

After her barrage of ideas, I told her, I said, "Mom, I'm not asking for your permission. I'm letting you know I'm out." She would tell me a few weeks later that she had to put that type of pressure on me. She said, "Rodney if you couldn't make it through my pressure, you wouldn't be ready for the world." She was right but I was ready. Well, I thought I was ready. I got an opportunity to perform at the world-famous PHAT Tuesday in Los Angeles at that time. Easily the best black comedy room in the country. Guy Torry was the host, the room would be full of the black Hollywood elite, celebrities, athletes, producers, etc. They would all be there to watch comedy and possibly to find the next guy. I had a set, I came down to LA, Angela and I hand in hand and we slept on my Aunt Lucy's floor.

Lucy's boyfriend, owned a Limo Company and when he found out I had a set that night, he dusted off the limo and we rode to the show. It was myself, Angela and about six other people that I did not know.

When you're with black people and you say you're a comedian, if they don't know you, they tell you one of two things. You better be funny or I hope yo ass is funny. I was still in the Navy and I looked like I was. I had no regular guy swag. My hair looked like the military. My clothes look like the military. Even though I had civilian clothes on, I looked military. We got there late. You see, they knew something that I didn't know, nothing starts on time in Los Angeles. I didn't know. I'm a Navy man, I make it to everywhere on time or early. I was late which created some anxiety in me. If there's one thing that's true about me it's that when I'm in uncharted waters or if I'm in a place that I've never been, that's the only moment I'm truly nervous. That day I was truthfully nervous. The worst thing you can be in a room full of black audience members is to be nervous. I walked on stage with my nerves all wound up and before I knew it, 30 seconds into my set, I was getting booed. A guy stood up to the left of the stage. A white guy. The only white guy in the audience stood up and booed me.

Then another person and another person. Before I knew it, I was being booed by everyone. I attempted to retaliate, tried to talk about this person and that person, nothing. Guy Torry came out and tapped me on the shoulder and said, hey man, you can't talk about my audience like that. He was right. I put my head down and walked off the stage. He proceeded to rip me. "I hope that guy didn't fly out here because he's not going to be able to get back on a plane with those bombs." He let me have it for five or six minutes and then someone in the audience said, "He didn't get a chance." Someone else said "he was only out there about 30 seconds" and then Guy said, "Do you guys want to see him again?" I stood there behind the sheer curtain, the curtain opened and Guy Torry asked me to come out. While this was happening, My wife was making her way to me. She made her way backstage. She asked me, "Are you okay?" Just as I answered her question, "I'm okay", the curtain opened and I was back on stage with Guy Torry. He said: "hey man, what happened?" I replied "I don't know." He said, "Do you want to try it again?" I quickly responded "Yes, I want to try it again." He said, "Alright, I'm going to introduce you again" and he gave me the best introduction. "Ladies and gentlemen coming to the stage show some love for Rodney Perry!" I walked out and immediately I jumped to my closing joke; my closing joke always worked.

I did the joke. On a scale from 1 to 10 may be the joke was a 7 at best. I took a deep breath and I said to the audience, "I think that's all I'm going to get out of you guys tonight. Thank you very much. My name is Rodney Perry." I walked off the stage that night and I knew more than I had known weeks before, that I had to leave the Bay area. I had to get to LA. I had to put myself in a pool of talented people that were more talented than I. At that moment, I made my decision for real. I wasn't reenlisting. I was going to be a real comedian. Angela and I packed up our things and we moved to LA.

Moving to Los Angeles. The first person we would meet was Johnny Andrews. We were apartment hunting and we went to an apartment building on Osage Avenue in Inglewood, California. Johnny was the Manager. Johnny and I began talking and we realized that our birthdays were days apart. He was a Virgo and I was a Virgo.

We became fast friends. Johnny suggested that Angela and I manage an apartment building. Hey, it's free rent. Sounded like a great idea. So, we did it. Managing that apartment building would turn out to be the worst job I ever had.

CHAPTER TEN
Leap of Faith

For every one that is contemplating taking a leap of faith. Take it, jump. Don't be afraid. However, I must warn you, on the other side of the leap of faith is real life. I had taken the leap, I leaped out of the Navy to the city of Los Angeles, California. I arrived in Hollywood and I got off the *I'm going to make it bus*, but I still had to take care of my family. I gained some valuable skills in the Navy and those skills would take care of us. First thing I did was join a temp agency. I remember the young lady; her name was Rhonda. Rhonda kept me busy. Well, with my clerical skills, I was very valuable doing data entry and providing secretarial services to different companies. When I wasn't doing temp jobs, I was managing an apartment building, actually three buildings. I said it was one of the toughest jobs I ever had and that was a fact. We managed three properties in Inglewood, California. That's three sets of accounting, three sets of distinctly different people. Three sets of light maintenance. I learned how to fix sinks and repair door jams. To be honest, Angela did most of that stuff, she is very handy.

One of my tenants was Donna. Donna would never take the liberty of getting dressed when I came by and she was always breaking something. She'd come in the bathroom with her housecoat on and ass sticking out. "Here you go Mr. Perry." "Ms. Donna please, put some damn clothes on, please!" I'm joking, but

I'm serious. She's was a great lady though. For the record, she wouldn't get dressed for Angela either.

I did temp work for many places. I spent some time in a modeling agency. I worked in a lawyer's office and I temped at the VA, the veterans administration. It was great to be around all these vets. I served in the Navy, so I understood what they were going through. While I was at the VA. I had been there maybe 10 days and in those 10 days, my work ethic shined through. They were considering hiring me. I got the word and to be honest, I was considering taking the job. It'd become very difficult to take care of my family. That's when I had the best conversation of my life. I had become friends with a Vietnam Vet. He and I would eat lunch together. He was a double amputee. He had lost his legs below both knees and we would talk at lunch.

He was doing data entry as well, but he was permanent. We were talking at lunch one day and he asked me, "Rodney, what are you doing here?" I said, "you know what I'm doing here, data entry?" He said, "No, dummy. Why are you in Los Angeles?" I said, "Well, I came to be a comedian, maybe an actor. I want to entertain the world." So, he asked me again, "Why are you here?" I thought about it. Why was I at the veteran's administration? Why was I contemplating maybe taking a full-time job there? I walked out of the VA that day. That was the last day I would work any job that wasn't comedy.

We all go through ups and downs. Your first time at anything is always amazing. My first television performance was on BET's Comic View. They recorded in Los Angeles, California at the Normandy Theater. I think Don DC Curry was the host. I performed that day and when I walked off the stage, my friend

Comedian Loni Love said, "Rodney, the way you spent that microphone was amazing." I must've had a mediocre set. The only reason you would ever compliment a microphone spin is when the guy had had a mediocre set. It wasn't horrible, but it wasn't great. The show wouldn't air for a few months, a few months pass, and my family and I took a trip to Chicago. The show is going to air while I was in Chicago. I was at my grandmother's house, my mother was there, my children were there, my wife was there, and we watched my television debut.

I was so excited. The show came on BET, National Television. I watched my set and crickets. That's right crickets. No, literally crickets. The producers thought it would be funny to drop the sound out and play crickets over your set. I was devastated. A national TV appearance and I had gotten the crickets. I was pissed. I was hurt. My cousins looked at me and were like, "maybe this comedy thing ain't for you." Maybe it wasn't, but I knew that it was. I wasn't the only one that got the crickets.

Quite a few people got them and it was horrible. There was one comedian, her name was Kathy Westfield. Kathy approached me. She knew I had gotten the crickets, she had gotten them as well. She said, Rodney, "that's bullshit. The way they treated us. We're going to sue them. We want you to join us." I was still upset. I was still hurt. I said, "hell yes, I'm in." I went home that night and talked to my wife, Angela Perry, Mrs. Keep it super real. I explained to her what we were thinking about doing, and she immediately said, "I don't think that's a good idea, Rodney. I mean, you might want to work with BET again someday. Maybe you don't want to burn that bridge." I thought about it and she was right. I didn't want to burn that bridge. So as quickly as I jumped on the bandwagon, I jumped off. Kathy hated me after that. I didn't really care. I wasn't wrong because I jumped off the bandwagon. I was wrong because I didn't tell her. I didn't go to her like a man and say, "Kathy, I've changed my mind. I'm not going to do that." I just didn't say anything. I said, absolutely nothing. Sometimes you have to be a man even when it's uncomfortable.

Joey Wells, Joey Kenneth Wells, one of my closest and dearest friends. I've learned more from this man that I've learned from almost anybody in my life. He is a member of Phi Beta Sigma Fraternity Incorporated. Through my relationship with Joey, I was able to see brotherhood. I was able to see how his fraternal network would always take care of each other. I was always impressed by that. Through Joey, I would see family. The way he dealt with his sister who has special needs or the way he took care of his mother, the way he, as a young father, mentored and took care of his son. Then I would learn how to be a comedian, how to dissect the newspaper and find that jewel Joey was always great at that.

I would also learn to cherish the things that you have. See, Joey grew up with not a lot and because of that, he cherished those things that he spent his money on, things that I might've taken for granted. Whether it was tennis shoes, or his car Joey treated them with the utmost care. Joey treated this car like it was a Rolls Royce and because I was his friend, I had access to that vehicle. The car was flossy. Joey, flossy and I rode everywhere. Joey had one rule. "Rodney, lock my doors." I failed him many times. Often times we'd be going somewhere, and I'd be in the car before Joey. He would look at me and say, "Rodney, how did you get in here?"

"I, I um, yeah, my bad, Joe." "Lock my door, Rodney!" This man rode me around for at least three years, if not more. Joey Wells took me everywhere I needed to go or wanted to go. The best thing about this is he never made me feel it. I didn't even realize it until I bought a new vehicle. I came to LA with two cars, a Dodge Neon and a Ford Taurus. The Ford Taurus got repossessed and the Dodge Neon got booted and I didn't have the means to retrieve it. I had no car, no transportation but it never felt like it because Joey Wells held me down. I will never forget him for that, and we were friends for a lot of reasons outside of that, but he's my guy because of that. I also learned from Joey resilience. He came to LA after quitting a lucrative position with City Year, a nonprofit that he worked for many years. He was doing God's work with City Year. He was helping young people become better people, but he had a dream. We all did.

I was already in LA, maybe a year when Joey arrived, I was managing an apartment building in Inglewood California. I rented Joey his first apartment. I gave him the keys to look at one of the units around the corner. It was at night. He said, "They are shooting down there!" I replied, "Oh my bad you should go down there during the daytime." Joey took it in stride and we were neighbors for quite some time. Joey Wells and Harry Ratchford are absolutely my best friends.

GMacK and the polyester players. GMack is a great figure. He is a jazz guitarist. He's an artist. Moreover, he respected the art of comedy. GMack had comedy rooms in Los Angeles. When Joey and I met GMack, he was running this band, the Polyester Players. Joey and I would get our first taste of Hollywood through GMack because GMack liked us for whatever reason. We'd walk into his events. He would introduce us like we were Jamie Foxx or Cedric the Entertainer. "Ladies, and gentlemen, show some love for Rodney Perry and Joey Wells in the building." It gave us instant clout and credibility.

In most places in LA at that time we were at the back of the line, Joey and I trying to figure it out.

I remember us standing outside the Hollywood Improv one night, Alex Thomas, Darryl Heath and Chris Spencer were kicking it. They were always having so much fun. They were a clique. We would look at each other and wonder, how do we get into a clique? What we learned later is that you don't get in to clique, your friends become the clique. Your friends become the group that people want to be around.

GMack started a comedy room at the Hollywood Park Casino in Inglewood, California. That was perfect for me because I lived in Inglewood and actually, I lived across the street from the Hollywood Park Casino. So those days when Joey couldn't pick me up for whatever reason, I could walk to the show and I did many nights. I walked to the casino. I would be there before the show started. People would host the show, Speedy, Tess Drake, Joe Blount, Brandon Bowlin just to name a few. I was always there though. The stage time was invaluable in LA. So, from time to time when a guy was late, GMack and Jaha, the young lady that was working with him would ask me "hey Rodney can you host till so and so gets here?" I would say "absolutely, I sure will", and I did just that. I hosted for them instead of somebody else time and time again until one day Jaha pulled me to the side. When I arrived early, she said, "Rodney, I owe you an apology. We're always leaning on you when other people aren't here, so I told GMack, why don't we just let Rodney host," and they did. I would make like $150 bucks a week, but more important than that was the stage time. I grew more on that stage than I grew in any other point in my career. I've had some great moments of comedy, but my time at the Hollywood Park, Casino with GMack, Jaha, MC Rock and myself is unparalleled. Unprecedented. Thank you, GMack.

At this point, I had three kids already and people would ask me, "Are you guys are going to have any more kids?" I would say, "yeah, if she keeps laying there." She kept laying there and we had another baby on the way. Raina Marie Perry. Raina was fair with little slanted eyes. She was a gorgeous baby. Six years had passed. I was just beginning to feel like financially, we're in a great place and then we became pregnant with Raina. I was flustered. I remember talking to my mom. I said, "Mom I've got a baby on the way. What am I going to do?" She shared this with me. "Babies come with blessings. That child is going to give you more blessings than you can count. You just prepare yourself for the blessings that this child is going to give you." She was right. Raina came with her own set of blessings.

Although I lived in LA, I would make frequent trips to the Bay Area because they would hire me as a headliner. I made a conscious decision when I moved to LA that I was no longer an opening act. I was no longer a feature. I was a headliner. Becoming a headliner is a mental paradigm shift. If you fail to make the shift in your mind, you'll never make the shift in real life. So, in LA, I was a bit of a rudy poot. In the Bay Area, I was a headliner.

There was a big competition that went on in the Bay. The Bay Area Black Comedy Competition and Festival. It yielded such big stars like Jamie Foxx, DL Hughley and Chris Rock. They had all graced, the Bay Area black stages.

People like Geoff Brown, Sheryl Underwood, Luenell, and Daniel Dugar all performed in the Bay Area Black Comedy Competition. The rumor was that Tony Spires, the producer of the show would manage certain comics and that comic was a shoe-in to win. Personally, I swore off competition. I felt like it was a bastardization of the art. How would you be an artist and be subject to the scrutiny of one person? Maybe I believed that because somewhere in my spirit or my soul, I didn't think I had what it took to win.

Then one day out of the blue, I get a call. It's Mr. Tony Spires, we had a lengthy conversation. We had a mutual friend that reached out to me and said, "Rodney, they want you in the competition." I said, "No" flatly.

Then Tony and I talked like two men. We talked about life. We talked about our respective journeys and I thought Tony was going to solicit to manage me, in which case the fix would be in and I would surely win. I even asked him, "Tony, do you want to manage me?" He was like, "no, Rodney, I do not want to manage you, man." He said, "Rodney, where you are you going I can't take you. I could get you booked in all the black shit everywhere, but you have that thing. You have that thing that can cross over and touch the world." After that conversation, I seriously considered performing in the Bay Area Black Comedy Competition.

The year was 2001 and I was headed to the BABCC. I ended up making it to the semifinal round, but the relationships I made were way more valuable than winning that year. The winner that year was a comedian by the name of Mike Bonner. I'll say this, Mike Bonner was more focused than any of us. Mike had just had a near-death experience and to look in his eyes was to look in the eyes of the person that was focused on another level. There was one moment we were in the green room together and I was joking around as I was preparing, and he was serious. He was focused. He had already won. You have to win in your mind before you can win in real life. I learned that in that moment.

One of the relationships I made was supremely valuable to me, I met Kelvin Bland. Kelvin Bland (KB) is Cedric the Entertainers' road manager. I was in the Bay Area and stayed with my friend, Darryl Wayne. He let me use his other car, so I had the run of his car and the run of Oakland. Thank you, Darryl Wayne.

One night after the comedy shows from the competition, KB asked me to give him a ride to the hotel. "No problem." Some girls overheard and asked for a ride too. I looked at KB. He was like, "yeah, let's do it." We took the girls to Oakland. I don't even remember who it was, but I remember trying to explain to them who this guy was. Kelvin Bland. "This is Cedric's road manager. You guys need to be nice to him." We dropped them off and KB looked at me and he said, "Rodney, you a cool dude. Man, I'm going to hook you up." I had heard that phrase before many times and I took it in stride. To be honest, I didn't think I would ever hear from him again. I dropped KB off at his hotel. It was the last day of the competition and we went our separate ways. About two weeks later I get a call. "Hey Rodney, its KB we want you to roll with us."

What? "What we want you to roll with us."

Wow.

Going on tour with Cedric the Entertainer.

CHAPTER ELEVEN
Welcome to the Business

Touring with Cedric changed my comedy career. Cedric showed us the possibilities. He had been touring with the Kings of Comedy and he did everything first class. You would be picked up at your home by a sedan. You would stay at the best hotels. It was classy. Our first dates were in Detroit and Indianapolis. I had a great set in Detroit, another great set in Naptown, so on my way home that weekend I sent KB a text.

I told him I had a great time and thanks for the gig. He immediately replied, "Rodney are, you available next week?" I said, "Yeah. Hell yeah. I'm available." Somebody had dropped out and I got another opportunity to roll with the king. The next two cities were Dallas and Houston. Dallas, Texas. Always a great city. We had a phenomenal show. Houston had a storm, so we were unable to go. For some reason, it made more sense for us to stay in Dallas than to go home early, so we stayed in Dallas.

Cedric took us out for a five-star dinner. Then we went to a Kid Capri party. It was unreal. Me, Lil Duvall, JJ Williamson and Prescott Gilliam toured that summer. I played all the best venues in the country, the Masonic Hall in San Francisco, the Fox Theater in Oakland, the Fox Theater in Detroit, The Murat theater in Indianapolis and Madison Square Garden just to name a few.

By the time a year had past, my confidence and my focus was at an all time. I was not only a comedian but I was a touring comedian. I went back to the BABCC that year. I won. My Mom said that the baby would bring blessings and she did. Now, time for some movies.

When we toured, in every city, there would be a contest with the radio stations. The winner of the contest got to open for the tour. In Los Angeles, the guy that won the contest is a guy you might be familiar with, his name is Kat Williams. Katt and I went back to my days in the bay area. We were longtime friends.

He had taken LA by storm and he had won that contest that night. I saw something in Katt that I have never seen in another comic. I saw a star.

At this point in his career, he had not arrived yet. Through some mix-up, Katt did not have a dressing room that night, but that didn't bother him. He commandeered a bathroom. He grabbed the sheet of paper and wrote a star on it and then his name Katt Williams. I saw that paper on the bathroom door and I said to myself, "wow, this guy is a star!" He knew when no one else did. Maybe 18 months later, Katt Williams was headlining the same venue on his own, how fast things change.

I realized fairly early in my career that if I wanted people to come to see me live, I needed to get on television or in film. I got a call to be in a film called *Livin' the Life,* a movie written, produced and directed all on a camcorder by a guy named Joe Brown. He said, "Rodney do you want to be in the movie?" I was like, "absolutely." I had never been in a movie. I showed up in Compton and Joe Brown was in his garage with all these index cards on a wall.

We shot a film. When the script called for crackheads, Joe Brown had real crackheads. The movie never amounted to much, but one of the scenes did go viral. A little kid cussing out an Asian lady in the corner store.

I got an opportunity to work with Barry Bowles and Brian Hooks. In the 90's these guys were in a tandem that made tons of low budget films. One of those films was called *Boogie Beach Bash*. The title was changed to *Malibooty*, both titles sound like porn, but it was good-hearted fun. I got to work with Brian Hooks and another up and coming actor, Brian White.

Malibooty was my first "real movie." I had a trailer and everything. Even though I was touring, I never stopped my weekly show at the Hollywood Park Casino.

One Thursday night I would meet a star. I noticed this lady, she kind of looked like actress Jackee Harry. No, it was Kym Whitley. Kym Whitley had a room in North Hollywood called the Haha Café, her and Buddy Lewis. Kym and I were cool, but this was the beginning of our relationship. I noticed Kym was funny, but I thought she could be even funnier. She did a set at the casino and I made some suggestions. She was taken aback that I would take the time out to give her a note for a set. The only person that ever helped her up to that point was Buddy Lewis. Kym had just got an opportunity to have her own show on BET. It was called *Oh Drama*.

Nowadays you see talk with women all the time. *Oh Drama* was the first show. This showcased African American women and Kym Whitley was at the helm. The budget was very low. She didn't even have a budget for writers, so Rodney Perry, Joey Wells, and Rodman became her writers. We would do her monologue and that was our focus at first. Because of Kim Whitley I learned my way around a television set. I also learned how to warm up an audience. Joey and I would take turns. We would keep Kym up in the wee hours of the night so we could run jokes by her. That was a great time. Kym Whitley gave me my first Hollywood job.

A bit of irony, the woman that was tasked with running *Oh Drama* was Marilyn Gill. Fast-forward many years we would work together again on the Mo'Nique show... small world.

Cedric and I had become friends and one day I got a call out of the blue. It was Ced. "Rodney, I'm about to do a TV show and I want you to be my warm-up guy." The show was Cedric The Entertainer Presents. He said, "I just don't want the usual suspects". See, there were a group of guys that did all the warm-up in LA at that time. He said he wanted some new blood. He couldn't give it to me outright but I would have an opportunity. They would shoot his show twice a week with the audience on Thursday and Friday. Because of my job with Cedric my time at the Hollywood Park Casino was coming to an end. I needed to find a new place to work.

That new place was the Comedy Union, a brand-new comedy club in Los Angeles. The man in charge was a guy from the Bahamas. His name was Enss Mitchell, a bit neurotic, but a love for comedy that would serve as the fuel that would power the Comedy Union for years to come.

Thursday and Friday, I would leave the set of Cedric's show and make my way to the Comedy Union to host my weekly show at 10pm.

To advertise the show, we began doing ads on KJLH, Stevie Wonder's station, kindness, joy, love, and happiness. It started with me going up there on Friday mornings to advertise the show for that night. One day became two days, two days became three days, and before I knew it, I was a permanent fixture on the morning show. Nobody ever offered me any money and a lot of people criticize me for going up there for free, but for me it made sense. I was building my brand. I was being embedded into the collective consciousness, so I showed up like clockwork every day.

The dope thing about working at a radio station owned by Stevie Wonder is that eventually, you will end up alone in a room with him. I was crazy nervous. He said to me, "You're the Virgo, right?" I replied, "Yes, Sir." Stevie is a Taurus. He said, "Look out the door and see who's talking down the hall." I leaned out the door and I said the person's name. He said, "I knew it." I was floored. He could hear their conversation clear all the way down the hall. I've got two words to describe Mr. Wonder, Super-Hero.

The best thing about Los Angeles is anything can happen at any time. A chance meeting could change your life. KB had become a bit of a Guardian Angel for me. The Cedric Show had ended. I ran into KB, I said "I know you guys are working on the movie, man. I need a movie." He said, "Rod, you know what? I've got you". He had told me that before. A day later I got a call to come in for an audition. The audition was for a movie called *Johnson's Family Vacation*.

I had an opportunity during pre-production to sit in on a table read for *Johnson's Family Vacation*. Was I going to be Cedric's brother? No, but I was going to be one of his cousins.

Jeremiah JJ Williamson and I got the nod. We were in Cedric's camp. We had toured with him and he gave us a shot in the movie. We both had lines. I actually worked the whole month on this movie. It was amazing. It was nothing like *Malibooty* because these people had money. Ced's manager, lifelong buddy, frat brother and friend, is Eric Rhone.

    I knew Eric because we toured with Cedric, he was right there every step of the way handling the business. About two weeks into filming *Johnson's Family Vacation* Eric pulls me to the side and said, "Rodney, you're doing a great job, man. We're really proud of you. You're doing an amazing, amazing job." I said, "thank you, Eric. Man, I really appreciate you guys taking a chance on me. That was awesome." He went on, "You know I manage Cedric, right?" I said, "Absolutely, man. I think that's dope. It is great that you guys are friends and also business partners as well." He said "Right, right. So, says he pays me 20% of everything he does." I said, "Right, I feel you." He said, "So, Rodney, we expect you to pay 20%." I replied, "Um, what?"

    I didn't understand, I mean these were the people that hired me. They are producing the movie. How could they draw a commission if they were producing? I was mad as hell. I was getting $2,500 a week. It was about 10 grand. I'd already done the math. Every penny was allocated for. I went home and talked to the lady that always had the right answer, Angela Perry. "What do I do?" She was mad too. She said, "Well, don't trip. You've just got to pay it." So, I began doing my research. I talked to some friends, asked folks about contracts, and the thing about paying commissions at the end of the year, you can always recoup that money in taxes.

So that's what I did. I saw him the next day. I was like, Eric, "I've got a check for you buddy. But first I need a tax ID number." I remember him looking at me like, oh, okay. The fact of the matter is you will pay somebody, might as well be your friends. To date, I've made thousands from my work in this film... Thanks, CED and the entire CTE family. Welcome to the Business Rodney Perry!

CHAPTER TWELVE
Domino

Our family continued to grow. We were blessed with another edition, Rihana Elizabeth Perry. Rhiana was a happy child and she might be the funniest of my children. She has a quick wit and a sharp tongue. We were living at the Osage apartments in Inglewood. Our tour as the managers had ended with the addition of Rihana. We moved into a three-bedroom apartment. It was like a mansion to us. My best friend, Harry lived right downstairs from us. He and I would battle on John Madden football daily.

Actually, even today, I still play the game. Harry and I had been on one of those all night, 24-hour binges, game after game after game. Angela was fed up. Instead of arguing with me to turn the game off, she turned the power off in the entire apartment. Harry packed up and went to his house and I went to lay down. I never thanked her. I think I was losing that game. When you're a comedian in Los Angeles, you're always performing at the Improv, the Comedy Store, the Laugh Factory or the HaHa Cafe. Where there was a stage, Rodney Perry was on it.

I had long since exorcized my demons from Fat Tuesday and I had become a regular there. On Tuesday night I had an epic set. I was phenomenal. The next day I'm in my three-bedroom apartment in Inglewood and I got a call. The person on the line said, "Hello." hey, this is Mo." I said, "Mo who?" She said, "Mo'Nique." I said, "Mo'Nique who?" She said, "Mo'Neeeek!". Oh my God. It was Mo'Nique from the Parkers, from television and film. She was calling me. She was calling me because she had seen me live, unbeknownst to me. She had been in the audience at The Comedy Store that night. She heard me tell stories about my wife and my family. She saw me be incredibly funny. We began to talk about comedy. She told me she liked my style, then she asked me a question. She said, "Rodney, don't take this the wrong way, but can I take your wife on a shopping spree?" I was floored by the offer and I said yes. A couple of days later, Mo'Nique's assistant arrived and took my wife to get whatever she wanted and or needed. Things to pamper her and things that were just needed in our home. She's spent upwards of $3,000 that day. I was overcome with emotion. I got her back on the phone and we talked. I asked her, "How do I repay you?" She said, "You don't repay me. Someday you'll bless some young comedian the way I'm blessing you."

That is Mo'Nique. I don't know what you've heard about her. I don't know what you think you know about her, but this lady is by far the most generous comedian I've ever met. Mo'Nique gave me some valuable lessons. I had worked with Ced the Entertainer and Steve Harvey, we were all men and with men there's always a quiet competition. With Mo'Nique and I, it was more like a brother and sister relationship. The first gig I did with Mo'Nique, she called me and said, "Rodney, I'm going to put you on the phone with the promoter." At that point in my career, I had never been on the phone with the promoter.

I said, "Mo'Nique, I don't even know what to say to a promoter." She replied, "Ask him for $5,000." I said, "Mo'Nique,

I've never gotten $5,000 to do anything." She said, "Just ask for it." ... and so I did. The man laughed in my face. He said, "I can get somebody here for $500 why should I pay you that?" I said, "man, you need to get Mo'Nique on the phone." So, he did. He called her immediately on three-way. "Hey Mo'Nique, your boy wants five grand." She said, "Hey Sugga well, give it to him." Then he said, "Mo'Nique, Nah, I can't do that now. You are willing to mess this deal up over 5,000?" she said, "No Sugga, YOU are willing to mess this deal up over 5,000!" The guy caved in and I got the $5000. Mo'Nique had broadened my horizons in one phone call.

With television, with becoming more popular, you get opportunities to perform on DVD. I performed on a DVD called *The Big Black Comedy Show*. I had a pretty good set on the show, and they were setting up to do another one. Ralph Farquar the executive producer offered me a set on another episode of *The Big Black Comedy Show*. He was poised to pay me more than I made the first time, but I turned it down. I told Ralph I wanted to do something else. I wanted to stand out. He said, "Well, I could make you a co-host", and he made me a co-host and who was my main host, Mo'Nique. That was the first time we would work together. Ralph often laughs at me because I took less money to do way more work, but at that point in my career, I was trying to build something that would make me stand out. I negotiated for them to put me on the cover of the DVD. I actually ended up on the back cover but it was a cover none the less. I thought that was important. *Johnson's Family Vacation*, a daily morning show on KJLH, and a successful comedy night at the Comedy Union my stock in Los Angeles was rising.

One day I get a call from Rushion Mcdonald. Steve Harvey was set to host the BET Comedy Awards and they reached out to me to become a writer. I went down there, and I did a couple of sketches with Steve Harvey and wrote for him that day. That would start a pretty good relationship between Steve, Rushion and I.

Steve had his show called Steve Harvey's Big Time. A writer position came open and I got that job. I had never written for TV before, but I was ready. Steve Harvey had a monologue and that was my responsibility, myself and Thomas Miles. It was a pretty relaxed atmosphere, but our boss Rushion ran it like we worked in white-collar America. He required that we be there by 9:00AM even though we actually didn't work until after 10. The lessons were invaluable. The game Rushion and Steve would give us was top notch. Often times Steve would stop and give Thomas and I words of wisdom. He asked me one day, "Rodney P, do you want this?" I said, "What do you mean Steve?" He said, "do you want this? I can't go to Applebee's with my family. I can't go to the mall without it turning into something else, so you have to ask yourself now when it doesn't matter, do you want this?" He'd drop jewels like that every day. Not only were we Steve's writers, but we would also get to sit in his office and be the fly on the wall while he conducted business. Everything from real estate to clothing. Steve was a mogul already. The man worked tirelessly. 5 am on the radio. From there, he would come to the set, work six or seven hours. That was impressive to me. His work ethic was unparalleled. From the set of *Johnson's Family Vacation*, Steve and I had become familiar with each other by playing dominoes. I must be honest; I was completely intimidated by who he was. The stature of a king, to face a man like Steve Harvey, head to head on Domino's was completely intimidating for a young comedian.

Steve had begun kicking my ass on the set of the *Johnson's Family Vacation* and he would carry those ass kicking's to *Steve Harvey's Big Time*. Steve would summon Thomas and me to his office, "Y'all Ready?" He would ask and he would proceed to put his foot knee deep in my ass. Steve and Tommy had a unique relationship. Tommy would talk cash shit to Steve. While I was intimidated, Tommy wasn't intimidated at all. Tommy had been working for those guys for a few years. He wasn't afraid.

I'm a Navy man for eight years. All I did was play dominoes. I knew I was better than this, so I went home one evening and I thought about it, there is no way this guy is beating me like this. I walked in the next morning and I was determined not to lose. I didn't initiate the challenge. I waited for him to call me and he did. I sat down at a small table, Steve and I face to face, man to man. I wasn't afraid. I won the first game quietly. I won the second game quietly. I looked at Steve and I said, "all right Steve, we should head back to work." He said, "No, y'all work for me. Sit down." We played another game and I won again. We played again and Steve began his theatrics. Every good domino player has a show. Steve began his show and I continued to beat his ass.

He finally yielded. I learned something about myself that day and I learned about life. If you're afraid, you can't do anything, even things that you do well. I had been afraid of Steve Harvey. I had been afraid of his stature. I had been afraid of the king, but when I was able to reduce him to a man and I was able to sit across from him, man to man. That was the most valuable lesson. Who knew? Domino's would teach me something.

Ralph the EP from *The Big Black Comedy Show*, gave me a call. They were shooting a new TV show and they asked Rodney Perry to be the host. Unbeknownst to me, they had already asked another gentleman by the name of Bill Bellamy to host that show. He had turned it down flatly and they came to me. I told them, let me sleep on it. Those are 5 words that I will never say in my life again. *Let me sleep on it*. I slept on it and I was slept on. Bill Bellamy came back and decided to host the show. They still liked my comedy, so they offered me another role. "We want you to be our man on the street." Never one to turn down a job. I said, yes. Rodney Perry, Bill Bellamy and Tommy Ford. We began shooting a show called, *Who's Got Jokes*? A comedy competition.

Who's Got Jokes? filmed for four seasons. We went around the country and I worked with some of the most awesome people in Hollywood.

Nobody really knew what my role would be on the show. They knew I would do man on the street stuff. They knew that I would be kind of Bill's co-host. Tommy Ford would be the moral authority on the show, but I had to learn while working on *Who's Got Jokes*, how to produce Rodney Perry, how to produce myself. In the first episode, there was a moment in the show where they introduced me, I came out in my underwear, some heart boxers with a robe on. Bill Bellamy said, "Ladies and gentlemen, Rodney Perry." He was genuinely surprised at the way I had come on stage. Bill asked, "what are you doing, man?" I thought we were starting later, man. I'm sorry, I wasn't dressed, but I just wanted to make sure I came out." That became a thing. Every show I would come out doing something different. By season four, it was a full part of the production. I did everything. They even asked me to come out with a lion.

Yup. A lion. We we're shooting that season in Las Vegas and Ralph had a friend that had a lion. My first thought was no. My second thought was no. My third thought was, hell no.

Siegfried & Roy had just had a horrific accident with a live animal, and they were professionals. I have no business dealing with a lion. So, I said no. Bill Bellamy told me, "say, Rodney, you don't want to be dealing with an animal when they do something they've never done." I said, "you're right." The compromise, I pitched that we used a stuffed animal as Martin Lawrence did on The Martin Show. They shot that down. Ralph was hell-bent on a live animal. He had a cat. A house cat. This cat was huge. It wasn't a lion, but it was one big cat. Rodney Perry, forever the team player. I said let's rehearse it. So, they gave me the cat and we were going through the bit and the cat literally ripped my shirt off. I handed the cat back to his handler and I told Ralph," I love you man, but I can't do it." We ended up doing the Martin bit I pitched earlier and it was funny.

We would also travel the country to find new comedians. I was on the road with *Who's Got Jokes* when I got a call from Rushion McDonald. You see, Steve would give me a gig every now and then, "Hey Rodney, Steve wants you to do a show in Charlotte, North Carolina" by that point, I was on TV myself. My stock had begun to rise.

Rushion asked how much I wanted for the show I said $2500. He said, "I don't know man let me look at the tickets. I'll get back to you." We played phone tag for a few days. Rushion came back to me and said, "Rodney, it's a done deal. We're doing the GIG." I said, "You never responded to the 2,500." He said, "Rodney, we've got $1200." We had gotten off the phone and my soul would not let me accept $1,200. In my mind we would settle at $2000 and maybe there was a reason he chose that number. I don't know, but I couldn't do it. I called him back. No answer. I sent him an email. I said, Rushion, first of all, thank you and Steve you all have been nothing but great to me, but I must respectfully decline this offer. I heard nothing. I heard nothing for years. They stopped working with me, but that was okay with me.

CHAPTER THIRTEEN
The Mo'Nique Show

Mo'Nique in the afternoon radio. I had done morning radio in Los Angeles on KJLH for four years. The entire time I was on that radio show, I never received any money. I was a glorified intern. I never tripped. It wasn't about money. It was about me growing the Rodney Perry brand.

One upside, I did get LASIK surgery for free. Don't get me wrong, there were some perks to being on air with Cliff Winston and the home team. Cliff was an awesome guy. Then there was Adai Lamar, Jerry El Nino, Janine Hydell, and Marc Keen. KJLH was truly a family. I was just the family member that wasn't getting paid.

So, when I got another radio opportunity, I was a bit gun shy. That opportunity came with Mo'Nique. Mo'Nique and I had become friends, but we would become closer. I gained a bit of celebrity in LA.

Barack Obama was running for office. Myself and a number of comedians in the area were asked to come and do a radio remote. It was a voting drive. That remote broadcast was for *Mo'Nique in the Afternoon*. I sat in with Mo'Nique that day and it was magic. She and I on the air were unadulterated fun.

We were like two kids, Mo'Nique, and Rodney Perry. We're great together. You never know when people are watching. You never know when you're needed. I had no idea at the time, but the gentleman that was co-hosting for Mo'Nique was about to leave. They needed a new guy. After sitting in with Mo'Nique, I was asked to come and sit in the studio as her cohost. I did. After the first day, I think it was a Wednesday, at the end of the day they said, "Rodney we'll see you tomorrow." I immediately went home and talked to my wife. I had done KJLH for several years without pay, and in my mind, this felt like the beginning of that.

Angela and I talked, I said "baby I don't want to do radio like this again for free." She turned and said to me, "Rodney, do you really think the woman that took me on a shopping spree, would have you work for free? Didn't she help you negotiate deals before? She wouldn't do that."

Again, Angela Perry with it; brutal, honest and sobering thought, but still the thought lingered in the back of my mind. Was this the beginning of another three or four years of free radio. Then came Friday morning, Then Friday afternoon. We did the show. It was magic. Once again, at the end of the day, Mo'Nique's husband, Sydney, pulls me to the side. I don't know if you've ever been pulled to the side, but it's never good. I went from thinking that I will be working for free to thinking that I was about to be fired. *How did you get fired on your day off, Craig?* The words of Ice Cube echoed in my mind. Sydney began telling me how much they enjoyed me on their show. He said, "We like you Rodney and we want you to join us." I didn't understand. He went on, "We want you to be on our team" but I still didn't get it. He said, "We want you to be Mo'Nique's Co-host Rodney. We can only pay you this much, he slid me a sheet of paper that had a number that was bigger than any number I'd ever seen. Then a grown man cried. I wept. That moment was a culmination of many years of work.

All the stage time, all the free shows, honing my skills and being ready for the moment. I was on the air. We had a blast. *Mo'Nique in the Afternoon* was nothing short of amazing. Mo'Nique is a great leader and I was an awesome co-host. Rob Wilkins, Kim Nelson Ingram, KDK Block, and Marcellina Olan, we were all members of a great team. We were making a fantastic show every day. I had taken that job, and, in my mind, Mo'Nique and I would rock this radio show for years to come. Five months later it was over.

The crazy part is I wasn't devastated. Sure, I was back out of a job, but I had been out of a job before. I walked away from the Navy for God's sake. Mo'Nique came to me after the show ended and said, "Rodney, bigger and better things are coming, don't worry baby." She was right. About two months later, I get a call. It was Mo'Nique. "Rodney got some big things coming, sugar! Can't talk right now but somebody is going to be calling you" and then she hung up. I didn't know what she was talking about, but I knew it was big. About a day later, I get a call from Sydney. "Hey Rodney, BET's going to call you. Mo'Nique just made the biggest deal in BET history. We're doing a late-night talk show. We want you to roll with us." Then he hung up! The next call I got was from a BET exec, "Mo'Nique wants you to join us. Are you willing to relocate?"

From my past. I normally would say, "Let me sleep on it", but I learned a lesson. I immediately said yes. I hadn't talked to my wife or anyone, but I knew I didn't have the luxury of meandering. "Yes, I'm willing to relocate." The exec said "that's fine, but we don't cover that. We don't pay for people to move." "No problem" I said, and the call ended. A few minutes later I received another call from Sydney Hicks.

"Rodney, did they call? "

"Yes, sir they called," I responded.

"Are you excited?" I told him "Man, I'm excited, but Sydney, they said they wouldn't cover my move." Immediately he says, "They said, what? Let me call you right back." People talk about Sydney Hicks. They say that he's ruining Mo'Nique's career. I have never seen my friend happier than I see her with this man. He's calm, he's collected. He's not at all a user or manipulator, in my opinion, and I've seen him up close. He called me back 15 minutes later. He said, "Rodney Perry is 20 grand enough to move your family across the country?" I said, "yes."

And just like that, we were headed to Atlanta. I was shooting *The Mo'Nique Show* and I'd had some experience with *Who's Got Jokes* and *BETs Comic View*, but this was different. This was on another level. This was a late-night talk show, and it was four nights a week. At the time we shot the show, Mo'Nique and I were the only two black people on television, period. *The Mo'Nique Show* was a God send. Two friends on camera having fun each night.

Atlanta is a good city. I had come to Atlanta many times over the years, whether it was for *Jamie Foxx's LaffaPalooza* or to come down and play the Uptown Comedy Corner, Atlanta was always a great city. I never saw myself living here though.

If you are famous in Los Angeles or have any celebrity, you are exponentially more famous in Atlanta. In the Atlanta streets, Rodney Perry was a star. That in itself was worth the price of admission. I realized quickly, shooting *The Mo'Nique Show*, managing my comedy schedule and any other business opportunities that came as a result of being on TV every night, I needed some help. Social media was beginning to bubble and my friend Royale Watkins had created a social buzz on Facebook. People were doing karaoke online. It was fun. One of the people that I would see during that time was a lady named Madeline. Madeline lived in Atlanta as well. She reached out to me online one day and said, "Rodney, I sent you a link. Take a look at it." I was busy. I was doing stuff. I didn't look at it. She asked me again, very kindly I might add. Rodney, "did you get a chance to look at that link?" I still hadn't looked at it. I was living my life. Taking care of the kids, my family etc. Finally, I took a look at it and what I saw floored me. This lady, this stranger had taken the liberty of creating a version of my website all on her own. I hadn't asked her to do it. What I appreciated the most was the initiative. She had redone my website and it was dope. Well done.

So, I took a meeting with her. We met face to face, and we talked. She was seeking a position with me as a publicist. I had some experience with publicists and I wasn't looking for a publicist at all. I don't discount the profession, but it's too vague for me. "I don't need a Publicist," I said, "but I do need your help."

Just like that, this lady came on board, a young white lady from Detroit, mother of three boys, cool husband. She was perfect. She had the swag of a black girl and the skin of a white girl. One of the kindest people I would ever meet. Madeline stepped into my life. She has been helping me navigate this entertainment landscape ever since.

When you're on television every day you buy things. After our first year on the air, I bought two cars the same day, a Camaro and a Chevy Yukon. Almost a hundred thousand dollars in one day, I was rich.

During that time, I also bought a home. The great thing about having a good woman in your life is they pray. Angela had put down a list of the things we wanted in a home. I had never seen the list, but when we moved to our new home in Smyrna, Georgia, she showed it to me. It was almost everything, she had prayed for our home to a tee.

Buying a house is the biggest investment you'll ever make. It was a daunting task. Angela and I looked at over 60 homes. Some things we liked, some things we didn't until we walked into this one, but we were outbid. We went to the place that we were renting, dejected and upset. Then God said your house is two doors away. The house popped up on the market. It had not been there the day before. A gentleman was living in his home by himself. His wife had left him alone in a five-bedroom home and he was reluctant to put it on the market. Suddenly he did. Our home magically appeared. I guess it wasn't magic, at all, it was a blessing.

Roxy Jordan Perry. My mother had said it many years before, "children bring blessings." Rachelle had gotten us out of the Navy and into an apartment in Inglewood, California. Raina had got us out of that apartment and into a nice two-bedroom apartment. When Rihana arrived, we went into a three-bedroom apartment, but Roxy would take the cake. Roxy's blessing was a five-bedroom house. I was on TV every night. I had cars, had a house and then ... *The Mo'Nique Show* was over.

We shot 300 episodes. We were greenlit for another 100 episodes. It was summertime. I was on the road and I get a call from the man, Sydney, "Hey Rodney. We've been put on indefinite hiatus. Get out there. Get your money, man." Indefinite hiatus? I didn't know what that meant. When a show is taken off the air there's a press release. There are news articles. No one ever said the Mo Show is canceled. Well, we haven't worked since that fateful day of indefinite hiatus. I guess the show can come back any minute. Now as I write this book, we've been off the air for about seven years. I have to be honest; I made more money with Mo'Nique than with any other comedian in the world. Mo'Nique made sure I made money on our tours and on our television show. We booked the tour, Mo'Nique and friends, Mo'Nique, Rodney Perry and Tone X. It was just us. I was used to getting $10,000 per show.

If we had 20 shows booked, that would be $200,000. That money would carry me for a couple of years. I took the deposit and began living life. I learned a valuable lesson: Don't spend the deposit. The business of that tour wasn't right for Mo'Nique and she ended up canceling that tour. That cancellation sent me into a financial spiral.

I mean, I was working, but I was never going to get the other half of that money. I had blown through the deposit and the gig wasn't going to happen, so I went back to the basics. I went to comedy clubs on my own. I had been working with Mo'Nique for the past four years or so. I had been on TV with 300 episodes, so I have some celebrity. I began building the Rodney Perry brand. I would travel around the country and play comedy clubs on the weekend, $2,500 bucks, $3,500 bucks, $5,000, or $1,000 sometimes too. I would do one nighters I would play black comedy clubs. I would play the mainstream clubs. When in doubt, tell jokes.

I went back to what I had always done, whether I was at the Hollywood Park or the Comedy Union, whether I was in a movie or on television. I was always a comedian, so I went back to the basics. Then another opportunity came, All-Star weekend. I was working with a lawyer. His name is Ricky Anderson. He represented people like Mo'Nique, Steve Harvey, Yolanda Adams and I was one of his clients as well.

They wanted to do a comedy special with me, Rodney Perry and Earthquake to shoot our comedy specials on the same date at NBA All-star Weekend in Orlando, Florida. We talked about the details of the special and I was to receive $30,000 for my show that day. It was surreal. I had movies, television, hosting and co-hosting gigs but this was special and for the first time the world would see my act. Specials make careers. It was an all-star weekend, the frenzy of Orlando, Florida. All the celebrities would be in the audience. I planned to do it big. I asked could I have a band. The production team said, "Sure, you can have a band, but you have to pay for it out of your own pocket. Rodney." I had some money. I had credit cards, so I paid for the band. It ultimately amounted to $9,000 in all to pay those guys. To get them there, to put them up in a hotel, but that was going to be nothing. It was a special. Comedically, I was absolutely ready. Emotionally I was not, I had no idea I would be so emotional the day I was shooting the special. I couldn't hold back the tears. I worked my whole career for this moment.

The crazy part, as I'm writing this book right now, nobody has ever seen the special. It was never released. All of my work. All of my tears and it was shelved as a result of some deal gone bad at Universal. Someday the world will see that special. It's funny if I do say so myself. I wanted a band. You can bet that I won't do that shit again. Well, at least I won't pay for it myself. That's for sure. It was a great band. Let me be clear. They were awesome, but it was an expense that I didn't have to incur.

CHAPTER FOURTEEN
Lessons

My career has been quite awesome up to this point, and we still pressed ahead whether it was being born to an unwed mother, whether it was Leo Jordan or Benjamin Perry. Rodney Perry or Mookie. You find your way. You find your passion. For me, that passion was and is, comedy.

I have my siblings. Sheri, Rion, JT, Charlie, Candy and Byron. I have a rich life from the streets in Chicago, 126th and State to 77th and Bishop. I was a Sandlot football legend. A lover of house music. I learned throughout my life that location is in everything. I lived in Monroe, New Orleans, Chicago, Los Angeles and Atlanta. Home is where your heart is. I have had great friends; Deitrick Mitchell, Michael Daniels, Alan Fisher, Harry Ratchford, Les Phillips. Roy Freeman and Joey Wells. I have known love; Octavia Turner, Alana Howard and most importantly, Angela Perry. I've had some wins and no losses. I have never lost, even when I hurt my knee.

In high school I wanted to be a starting full back, so bad. I hadn't lost. Wow. Standing outside the Regal Theater and listening to a comedian named Robin Harris demolish the crowd. Through that moment, I would get a glimpse into my own journey.

My mother would be there with me every step of the way. She's was my friend, my confidant, and even though she has gone to be with God now, I still feel her with me.

Life is ripe with peaks and valleys. Whether it's my Navy career, my comedy career, or my career as an apartment manager, it's all been amazing. I am a comedian. However, the role I cherish most is that of a father. Hope Latasha Hartwell, Devin Devante Harris, Rachelle Perry, Raina Perry, Rihana Perry and Roxy Perry, they are my legacy. There are so many meetings, so many people that affect you. Comedians like Tony Royster who told me, "Rodney, take your stuff out of your pockets before you go on stage it's distracting." Or the VA vet that asked me that life changing question, "what are you doing here?" Friends like Joey Wells that held me down when I couldn't hold myself down or GMack, the mentor I needed at that moment.

So many people: Kim Whitley, Stevie Wonder, Cedric the Entertainer, Steve Harvey … they all played a role in shaping the man sitting here today. Angela Perry; as I reflect now, this woman is absolutely the best person in my life. I am a better human because of her. She has always had my back regardless of our situation, whether we had money or not, whether we had things or not, she is and was always there.

Okay. Okay. Okay.

I'm a touring comedian on the road 25 weeks a year. Not making a lot of money, but making some money, doing good. Maintaining my lifestyle. Not living beyond my means. I was beginning to feel like I wasn't healthy. I couldn't run anywhere, but I attributed it to being tired. I just have to work.

The American Heart Association and American Stroke Association use an acronym. The acronym is F.A.S.T. F.a.s.t is used to identify strokes: **F**ace drooping, **A**rm weakness, **S**peech slurring. If you notice these things, it's **T**ime to go to the hospital. I had been pretty busy. I was in Charlotte, North Carolina one night, then back home to Atlanta and then I was headed to Denver, Colorado. There were riots in Charlotte during that time. I did the engagement in Charlotte and went home. One day I was on the phone talking to Madeline and as I was talking to her, my speech slurred. I wasn't aware of F.A.S.T at that time. If I were, maybe I could thwart off the impending stroke. Another symptom that you may be in trouble is a condition called toe drop. Your toe would drop below horizontal and it will cause you to slip or, stumble. Your balance is off. I was experiencing all that. Plus, I had gained far too much weight. I was 270 pounds and unbeknownst to me, I was in trouble.

I arrived in Denver, Colorado for an engagement at the Denver Improv. It was a Friday. I had two shows that night. I had my PlayStation on the road with me so I played a couple of games with my friend Sydney Castillo. I beat Sydney that day. I took a call from Joey. He was informing me that a friend of ours, Mickey Gordon, had suffered a stroke. As he told me what she was going through, I was worried about her and myself.

In my mind's eye, I remember saying to myself, I feel like that now. The next conversation I had was with Hank Denson. He's about as close to a doctor as you want to deal with, without talking to an actual doctor. I told him how I was feeling and he immediately said, "Rodney, go get your blood pressure checked." I got myself together and I dragged myself across the street to Walmart. I went into the pharmacy department and I put my arm in the sleeve. My blood pressure that day was 221/140. An old lady walked past and glanced at my blood pressure and said, "Oh baby, that's high." I wanted her to mind her own business. If I would have gone to the hospital right at that moment, again, maybe I wouldn't have had the stroke. But I didn't. You see I'm a comedian. I needed the money from the gig to take care of my family and I had to fulfill my obligation.

To be honest, I really had some morbid thoughts that day. I knew I was in trouble. I remember thinking to myself, if I'm going to die today, I want to die on stage. So, I went and did those two shows. My feature act that weekend was a man by the name of Rion Evans. Rion Evans is my brother.

Rion and I had become a bit estranged. He was upset with me and I was upset with him. We weren't really talking, but we absolutely love working together. I told him that I wasn't feeling great, but we could go to the VA after the shows that night. So, I went up and performed in Denver, Colorado. I'm sure I was affected by the altitude as well. I delivered a fantastic performance, if I say so myself, but I wasn't myself. I leaned on the wall the whole time. The normal physical and energetic Rodney Perry was delivering some gut-busting laughter from a stationary position. I shook hands. I took pictures and then we went to the emergency room, not urgently I might add. To be honest, I thought I would go to the VA. They would lower my pressure and send me home. You see, I knew I was hypertensive. They'd given me medication years before but I elected not to take it.

The medication affected my libido and that was something I wouldn't tolerate. So, five years later, no medication.

Blood pressure's through the roof. I drag myself into the Veterans Administration hospital. This time, I'm not doing data entry. I'm a patient. Those moments are a bit of a blur for me. I was having a stroke. I walked into the hospital but I would not walk out for some time.

I remember them working on my heart that night. A doctor with a handlebar mustache talked to me as he examined me. He told me my heart had become thick. You see, if you are in the realm of stroke, your heart is probably in trouble as well. I was like an old car that was running hot. I spent the next eight days in ICU. My speech was slow. My face was distorted. I lost the use of the left side of my body. I had a stroke. My birthday had just passed. I was 46 years old and now it was time to work.

It's interesting how God works. Yes, I had a stroke, but ironically enough, the Denver VA was the home of the #1 stroke rehab facility in the VA system. The best care. I received that.

I talked with God a lot during that time. I asked "God, why me?" God responded, "Why not you?" I asked God, "What am I to learn?" He told me, "You spent your whole life trying to get to something way out in the distance and now you are a man that cannot even take a single step." He said, "Understand this Son. The ability to take that step is a success."

My brother Rion was there every step of the way, every single day. To reflect on it now, it makes me emotional. Yes, we had our differences. He didn't allow that to stand in the way of him helping me. Whether it was a run to Walmart or him just being there to play a game with me or talk to me. He sat with me every day. Eight days in ICU and then 40 days of rehab. I was in the biggest fight of my life.

I have been in head to head combat before and folded under the pressure, but this fight was the toughest fight I would ever be in and I was determined not to lose. I was fighting for my family, for my friends. I was fighting for my loved ones. I was fighting for my position.

I was fighting without the use of my left side. The rehab process was grueling. If a heart attack happens to the heart, a stroke is a brain attack. No use crying over spilled milk. I went through the rehab process.

The nursing staff took great care of me. They would wipe me up and made sure I was clean. When you can't use one side of your body, it makes it really hard to wipe your butt. I was in a wheelchair. I would graduate from the wheelchair to a walker. I would then graduate from the walker to a cane and then from a cane to walking on my own. Almost 50 days later, I walked out of the hospital a changed man. A new man. Rehab doesn't end when you leave the hospital. Now you've got to go home. People are living their lives. People are working. You have to navigate your home. You have to scale the steps. You have to get back on the madden sticks. My buddy TuRae Gordon and I had become fast friends, our daily games of Madden were epic. While I was in the hospital, he stopped playing the game because of me.

As I think about it, I actually got a chance to die and come back because as I laid in my hospital bed, with a stroke, I was able to see all the things that happen when you die. People posting pictures of me. They were saying little anecdotes I had shared with them over the years. They were posting their relationship with me as if I was gone. I got a call when I was in the hospital, "we want to do a benefit for you." I told them, "No. Benefits are for dead people." I wasn't done yet.

So now I'm back home. Although I went back on stage immediately. It took me almost two years to get my balance back fully. Up to this point in my life, I was o-3 in fights. I finally won a fight, I kicked that strokes ass!

To go through everything I went through with my stroke is one thing. To lose the central figure in my life, is another. My mother, Venice Celeste Hunt Perry Evans Coleman was diagnosed with a condition called COPD, Chronic Obstructive Pulmonary Disorder. It's a breathing disorder exacerbated by years of cigarette smoking. I don't think I ever considered the word chronic until the end. The moment you get this diagnosis, the clock starts. She knew none of us wanted to consider it.

You think you understand but you don't. I didn't. Through my life, I had friends to lose parents or loved ones and I tried my best to be there for those people. After losing my mom, I understand that I wasn't there. You don't know until you know. You won't understand until you understand. Losing a parent is something else. I remember as a boy telling my mother, "Momma, I don't ever want to see you die. I want to die first." She'd say, "Rodney, don't be a fool. Parents should never have to bury their child. I'll be gone one day. Rodney, you have to do this without me." My mother was always preparing me for the inevitable. You see, she not only was my mother, but she was my friend as well. We had grown up together. She had me at 19.

The last days the COPD was running its course and I urged my Momma to let me take her to the hospital. She said "I don't want to go to the hospital. If I go to the hospital Rodney, They're never gonna let me out." She was right.

I've always been a spiritual person, but I did not understand God until I looked at my mother's lifeless body. She had been in the hospital for a week or so. I reached out to my siblings and said, "Get here if you want to say your goodbyes. Get here." And they did. We were together for the first time in many years as we said our goodbyes to our mother. We made our peace. She did not go until we were all there. The medical professionals had done all they could do, and they advised us, It was time for her to go to hospice to make her comfortable. So, we did. We all sat around her in the room. It had been a long day. We left the hospice and I went home and laid down.

As I laid in my bed, I fell asleep. While I was sleeping, I saw a bright light and then I was awakened. Hank and his wife Jessie had stopped by to check on us. As I was talking to them on my back porch, I got a call. "Hello, Mr. Perry. She's gone." I asked the lady on the phone, "When did it happen? What time?" She said, "about seven minutes ago." Seven minutes ago? I wonder, was that the moment I saw that light? I think it was. I jumped in the car, rolled across town to the hospice facility and I looked at my mother's body. My mother wasn't dead. Well, she was, but she was gone. The thing that animates us had left her body. You might call it the Holy Spirit, you might call it her soul, and whatever that thing is. It had left the building. I didn't feel like she no longer existed. I felt like she had left that vessel and it was empty. It was like looking at an empty house, looking at her body, lying in bed. She was just not there anymore.

I have my tears. Those are my tears. I miss her but I know my mother is happy. She's in a great place. She's where she always wanted to be, with God. She gave me countless lessons over the years. "Rodney children come with their own set of blessings. Be a leader son. Don't be a follower." She had a concept called divine delay. She always said, "Rodney when you're being held up, sometimes you're being held up for reason. You're always where you should be at the moment. You should be there. That my son, is a divine delay." Finally, I understood what Dr. King was talking about. He said, "I'm not afraid as I write this book today, I'm not afraid. I'm not afraid of what the future holds. I'm not afraid to be a man. I'm not afraid to be a father. I'm not afraid to win, and I'm not afraid to lose."

I'm thankful for every moment. The good moments, the bad moments, the great moments, the sad moments. I'm thankful for every moment on my journey and the journey is not over, but this book is.

ABOUT THE AUTHOR
Comedian Rodney Perry

Rodney Perry is a Comedian, a Husband, a Father and a Stroke Survivor among other things. Over 20 years in entertainment has afforded him the opportunity to see the world. Whether he is cracking jokes on the comedy stage, creating and producing content for television, punching up a script or conducting business as the CEO of RP Live Entertainment, RP insists on always remaining kinetic.

Made in the USA
Lexington, KY
24 October 2019